'This book expertly and elegantly weaves tog
affective and the political in a forceful enga
racism in the academy. The strength of the boc
intersectionality and, especially, its focus on wo
the book is a must-read for all scholars and st
affected by the British academy's racialized environment.'

**Professor Robbie Shilliam, School of Politics and International Relations,
Queen Mary, University of London**

'The testimonies of women of colour in the academy have tended to
remain in the shadows, whitewashed by the structures of the Ivory
Tower, dismissed as anecdotal evidence rather than acknowledged as data
indicating individual and structural forms of exclusion. This timely book
starkly captures what the recent metrics of under-representation of women
of colour actually mean in academia. It amplifies the nuances of experience
at the same time as encouraging agency in the face of tenaciously
resistant-to-change systems of privileged activity. It is essential reading for
anyone genuinely interested in improving the conditions of all women in
contemporary higher education.'

Professor Vicky Gunn, Glasgow School of Art

'Academic life is punctuated by dissenting voices challenging the hegemony
of stultifying, racialized patriarchies. This pioneering collection draws on
critical race studies to centre the marginalized female voice, which is in
constant conflict with an education system that at one level understands
gender disparities while at the same time reducing the protests of women
to privileged identities easily identifiable in the eyes of the most influential
stakeholders – White, middle-class, straight men. The authors in this
collection should be applauded for their critical insight and transgressive
methodologies, yet the parochialism of the academy is evidence of border
maintenance and backlash politics. Whose voices should be privileged?
The myth of educational meritocracy is brought into question when the
voices of Black women are denied. The desire for intellectual and political
syntheses should be consistently welcomed in the academy and it is in this
spirit that all should welcome as an essential text the important stories of
Black women academics and their lived realities in the Ivory Tower.'

**Professor Kevin Hylton, Head of the Diversity, Equality and Inclusion
Research Centre, Leeds Beckett University**

Inside the Ivory Tower

Inside the Ivory Tower

Narratives of women of colour surviving and thriving in British academia

Edited by Deborah Gabriel and Shirley Anne Tate

 is an imprint of

First published in 2017 by the UCL Institute of Education Press, 20 Bedford Way, London WC1H 0AL

www.ucl-ioe-press.com

British Library Cataloguing in Publication Data:
A catalogue record for this publication is available from the British Library

ISBNs
978-1-85856-848-5 (paperback)
978-1-85856-849-2 (PDF eBook)
978-1-85856-850-8 (ePub eBook)
978-1-85856-851-5 (Kindle eBook)

Typeset by Quadrant Infotech (India) Pvt Ltd
Printed by CPI Group (UK) Ltd, Croydon, CR0 4YY
Cover image ©Hybrid_Graphics/Shutterstock.com

Contents

Dedicated to Black feminists past and present

On sisterhood, solidarity and self-empowerment
Deborah Gabriel

Because of sisters who came before us, we are free

To challenge the Eurocentric mentality,

We're free to express our frustration, we're free to complain

As empowered women, our resistance will never wane.

From a Black feminist standpoint, we analyse and critique,

Through sisterhood and solidarity, we expose the mystique;

We unpack the mechanics of raced and gendered discrimination, micro-aggression and victimization,

Together we share strategies for survival and success,

Through narratives of our experiences we bear witness.

Our aim is not only to promote solidarity,

But maintain the tradition of activism, so other women can achieve.

So I thank you my dear sisters for your courage, strength and honesty,

Your inspiring words, your wisdom and your loyalty,

They help to keep faith and hope alive so that we can all continue to thrive.

Notes on contributors

Claudia Bernard is Professor of Social Work at Goldsmiths, University of London. Her research interests lie in investigating the intersection of race, gender and social class with child welfare, and she is interested in developing research methodologies that open up new ways for understanding violence and abuse in the lives of children from marginalized communities. She has written widely on child abuse; publications include *Constructing Lived Experiences: Representations of black mothers in child sexual abuse discourses* (Ashgate, 2001) and an edited collection entitled *Safeguarding Black Children: Issues for social work policy and practice* (Jessica Kingsley Publishers, 2016).

Jenny Douglas is a senior lecturer in health promotion in the Faculty of Wellbeing, Education and Language Studies at the Open University. She has a PhD in Women's Studies and her research is wide-ranging, spanning issues around race, health and ethnicity across 30 years. The key theme unifying her research and activism is intersectionality – exploring how race, class and gender affect particular aspects of African-Caribbean women's health. Dr Douglas is an honorary member of the Faculty of Public Health and a research affiliate of the Institute for Intersectionality Research and Policy, Simon Fraser University, Vancouver.

Deborah Gabriel is a senior lecturer at Bournemouth University in the Faculty of Media and Communication. Her research interests are focused around political communication and discourse; raced and gendered constructions and representations in media and popular culture; equality, inclusion and liberation in educational practice; and the dynamics of race, ethnicity and culture in higher education. Dr Gabriel specializes in delivering programmes of curriculum diversification and inclusive teaching practice through social justice pedagogy. She is the Founder and Director of Black British Academics, an independent network aimed at tackling racial inequality in UK higher education, and currently serves as Deputy Chair of the Race Equality Charter Committee at Bournemouth University.

Ima Jackson is a lecturer at Glasgow Caledonian University in Scotland and an experienced clinician, researcher and project manager. She has spent most of her career working with marginalized groups, including pregnant women in the poorest parts of London and Glasgow, and more recently refugees, asylum seekers and other migrants in Scotland. Dr Jackson's migration research, practice and policy focus comes from engagement with migrant communities, and she seeks to develop and embed within organizational and policy changes the experience of those who have migrated.

Josephine Kwhali is a senior lecturer at Coventry University and Course Director of the Social Work undergraduate degree. Prior to entering higher education, she held senior management positions in London borough councils, including as Assistant Director in Lambeth, Hammersmith and Fulham, Head of Children's Resources in Greenwich, and Head of Children's Services in Hackney. Dr Kwhali was awarded her doctorate from Sussex University, exploring the narratives of African-Caribbean Christian elders and Black theology's contribution to anti-racist social work. She acknowledges the sacrifices of those who have made her life and understandings possible.

Heidi Safia Mirza is Professor of Race, Faith and Culture at Goldsmiths, University of London. She is known for her pioneering intersectional research on race, gender and identity in education. She is the author of several bestselling books, including *Young, Female and Black*, which was voted by the British Education Research Association (BERA) as one of the top 40 most influential educational studies in Britain. Her other publications include *Black British Feminism* and *Race, Gender and Educational Desire: Why black women succeed and fail*. Her most recent co-edited book is *Dismantling Race in Higher Education: Racism, whiteness and decolonising the academy*.

Elizabeth Opara is Head of the Department of Applied and Human Sciences and an associate professor in the Faculty of Science, Engineering and Computing at Kingston University, London. Her area of expertise is nutritional biochemistry and she is a co-leader for the Sport, Exercise,

Nutrition and Public Health Research Group. She also contributes to the development of burgeoning nutritionists as a registration and continuing professional development assessor for the Association for Nutrition. Dr Opara has worked as an academic for almost 20 years and uses her experience in higher education to mentor staff as part of Kingston's 'Beyond Barriers' mentoring scheme.

Aisha Richards is an academic and creative practitioner whose research interests are focused around social justice in higher education. She developed and currently directs Shades of Noir, a programme centred on race in creative arts education and industry delivered across the University of the Arts London and other institutions within the UK. Through Shades of Noir, Ms Richards has developed strategic and holistic approaches to cultural change, with an emphasis on social justice, in all areas of higher education. These draw on collaborative strategies that engage staff and students at all levels and which support collective transformation.

Shirley Anne Tate is the first Professor of Race and Education in the Carnegie School of Education at Leeds Beckett University. Her primary area of research is Black diaspora studies broadly, and her intersectional research interests are institutional racism, the body, affect, beauty, race, performativity and Caribbean decolonial studies. She is also a visiting professor and research fellow in the Institute for Reconciliation and Social Justice, University of the Free State, South Africa, and a research associate in the Centre of Critical Studies in Higher Education Transformation at Nelson Mandela University, South Africa.

Marcia Wilson is an associate dean in the School of Health, Sport and Bioscience at the University of East London (UEL). She has a PhD in Sport Psychology from the University of Iowa, USA, and has taught and researched higher education for more than 25 years. Her research interests focus on social justice in sport and education. She is the Race Equality Charter Mark champion for UEL and is a mentor to both staff and students. In April 2016, she was awarded the 'Pay It Forward' Inspirational Woman Award for her work with athletes and students.

Introduction

Deborah Gabriel

This book has its origins in the Black Sister Network – a platform created within Black British Academics (a network of academics committed to tackling racial inequality in higher education) for women of colour. It was conceived as a space to provide much-needed mutual support, understanding and refuge from our day-to-day oppressive experiences within academia. Black Sister Network was, and is, more than a space of shelter in which to lick our wounds – it is a site of resistance through which we aim to fulfil our mission: to build solidarity and engage in collective activism; to develop strategies (collectively) to overcome exclusion and marginalization; to explore and articulate our experiences through counter-narratives; and to undertake research around race and gender using critical approaches. This book was developed as a means of combining all the elements of our mission into a single, collaborative project, back in October 2014, and it is immensely rewarding to us all that it has finally been completed.

The narratives within this book represent a journey that we – as women of colour, and as sisters connected by shared histories and experiences of raced and gendered oppression – embarked on together. This journey is not complete; it is an ongoing mission as we reflect on our reflections and discuss ways of moving forward. One thing that is clear to all of us is that this book was always a political mission rather than an academic exercise. As the narratives reveal, we can choose to assimilate into an organizational structure and institutional space that was never created for us, and adopt the dominant social norms with the hope that our compliance will be rewarded – or we can choose, in a myriad of ways, to resist. We choose to resist – and this book is a collective act of resistance.

To say that women of colour are under-represented in British higher education is to state the obvious. You don't need to review the latest figures from the Higher Education Statistics Agency to know that we are few in number. Just visit any university campus and you will find few Black and Brown women in the lecture halls, seminar rooms, shared offices and staff rooms – and fewer still in single-space offices, denoting seniority. However, the focus of this book is not about under-representation, it is not about 'diversity' and the need for 'more diversity' or for more Black and Brown bodies in White spaces (Ahmed, 2009), even though that would be welcomed. Our focus here is on highlighting the lack of regard for 'race' in discussions around gender equality and the exclusion of 'race' when examining women's experiences as academics in Britain. As women of colour we are the hidden minority in discourses around gender equality. Refusing to acknowledge the experiences of women of colour in academia contributes to our invisibility and serves to perpetuate raced and gendered discrimination. The time has come to stop adding women of colour to gender equality agendas embedded within ideologies, policies and practices that have been constructed around Whiteness. By excluding Whiteness from discussions about gender equality, there is little hope of the institutional cultural change necessary to bring about social justice and equality – which should be the aim of equality agendas, rather than seeking to 'add diversity' to existing structures that reinforce White privilege. 'Race' must be considered from the outset and understandings of discriminatory practices in higher education must be informed by our experiences because, as the narratives reveal, raced and gendered discrimination has become so normalized that it largely goes unnoticed – except to those of us who experience it.

This book therefore places the perspectives, experiences and career trajectories of women of colour in British academia at the centre of analysis. It positions academia as a space dominated by Whiteness and patriarchy, where women of colour must develop strategies to survive and thrive amid raced and gendered discrimination. We explore and analyse, largely but not exclusively through Black feminist theory, how our experiences as women of colour in British academia are shaped by race and gender. We reflectively explore and analyse how racism manifests in our day-to-day experiences within faculties and departments, from subtle micro-aggressions to overt forms of raced and gendered discrimination. Our findings are presented as a selection of autoethnographies, which touch on common themes such as invisibility, hyper-visibility, exclusion and belonging, highlighting intersectional experiences.

While there are common themes that run through our narratives, which suggest that other women of colour may have had similar experiences, these narratives are not presented as 'proof' or 'evidence' of some standard mode of raced and gendered discrimination. Instead, we present our stories as subjective realities, which represent 'theoretical interpretations' of our 'reality' as women 'who live it' (Collins, 1990: 22). These interpretations are deliberately drawn from a selection of women at various levels within academia, from lecturer to professor; and this is important, since career advancement provides no indemnity from racism and its specific intersections with other factors such as gender, ethnicity and class. It is misguided to think that as women of colour all we seek is career advancement because, as the narratives reveal, experiences of raced and gendered discrimination do not disappear because of a promotion – they persist at all levels, so the only solution is cultural change.

Within discourse around equality and diversity, 'institutional culture' is often framed in abstract terms that ignore the ways in which individuals perpetuate White privilege by implementing procedures and policies that produce disparate outcomes for people of colour. Diversity agendas also neglect to interrogate attitudes, behaviours and actions that perpetuate raced and gendered discrimination. This book therefore aims to highlight the nuances and complexities of how Whiteness plays out in day-to-day interactions and experiences through our lived realities. Our aim is not to invoke sympathy, but to help readers of all ethnic backgrounds develop a critical consciousness so that they are better able to recognize the subtle but impactful ways that raced and gendered discrimination occurs through membership of a racial/ethnic group, and how racial/ethnic identity has material consequences in terms of privilege or disadvantage. It is only through the development of a critical consciousness that the attitudes and behaviours of individuals that perpetuate Whiteness and contribute to unequal power relations will change.

While the narratives in this book are presented as a collective act of resistance against our marginalization as women of colour in British academia, they are also individual stories shared by brave women who agreed to bare their souls to inform and educate some readers and inspire and empower others. We are diverse in ethnicity, age, socio-economic background and geographical location and are drawn from a range of disciplines. We are not all social scientists, sociologists or educationalists – but we all make important contributions to this book. Some writers have adopted Black feminist theory for the first time in their lives, trying to make sense of their individual experiences and to place them in a broader context to build on what Black feminism has already contributed to the understanding of raced and gendered experiences. This project was never about assembling a team of Black feminists to theorize the experiences of others – it was always aimed at providing an opportunity for women of colour who work in British academia to empower themselves by participating in a collective research project centred on discursive activism. We take pride in this approach, which is influenced by the values of Black British Academics, in terms of building intellectual and social capital within our communities and highlighting our contribution to the global knowledge economy.

These narratives reflect high and low points in our professional lives as academics; however, although centred on academia, these stories do not occur in isolation from other raced and gendered social experiences of women in British society. It is important to note, when examining intersectional, racialized experiences, that academia does not exist as an impenetrable bubble but as part of a wider society where race, gender and power are interwoven, and raced and gendered ideologies, attitudes and behaviours are transferred through and within its boundaries.

We hope readers will find this book illuminating and that it will take you out of your comfort zone – to promote reflection and dialogue as a catalyst for change.

References

Ahmed, S. (2009) 'Embodying diversity: Problems and paradoxes for Black feminists'. *Race Ethnicity and Education*, 12 (1), 41–52.

Collins, P.H. (1990) *Black Feminist Thought: Knowledge, consciousness, and the politics of empowerment*. London: Routledge.

Chapter 1

The accidental academic

Josephine Kwhali

Introduction

In describing the divided self-perception experienced by Black people living within a White cultural context, Frantz Fanon (1986) spoke of 'Black Skin, White Masks'. He explained that in order to survive within settings that embody White cultural norms and ways of being, Black people are required not simply to adopt behaviours, attitudes and values that may be at variance with their own experiences of race, but to accept those behaviours and values as normative and, indeed, desirable. However, as Black people continue to be Black, the adaptation will always be partial. This is not only because skin colour provides a marker of difference, but also because values, experiences and culture will continue to be shaped by the historical and colonial relationship between White people and people of colour and by the contemporary racism that underpins it. Fanon discusses the psychological consequences of acquiescing to White dominant norms and the dependency it creates in Black people for White approval.

Fanon's work was to the forefront of my thoughts as I began to reflect on my own professional journey – a journey that has led to a seemingly successful career but where complex issues of identity, belonging, racism and cultural assimilation have consistently featured. It is a journey of contradiction and of enigma, of celebration and of hope, of pain and of joy. It is a journey that I share with thousands of other Black British women and it is a journey that is uniquely mine. It is a journey that I continue to travel along, in the knowledge that I will never entirely reconcile the personal and political meaning of my race, class and gender within a higher education setting constructed around the epistemology of Whiteness, maleness and class divisions. In recognizing this reality, I have perhaps come a little closer to deconstructing the White mask and acquiring a more informed understanding of who I am, rather than what the academy might wish me to be. This chapter is the story of that journey from schoolgirl to university academic. It is a story that embraces education in its widest sense: formal schooling, the hidden curriculum that privileges White knowledge and world views, political knowledge and international insights, and the experiential education arising from life experience, reflection and struggle.

Setting the context – visible yet invisible?

The House of Commons Home Affairs Committee report on police diversity revealed that only 5.5 per cent of officers are from a Black or minority ethnic background, although Black and minority groups account for 14 per cent of the population, and representation at senior levels is even lower still (House of Commons Home Affairs Committee, 2016). While the government and the College of Policing have clearly identified the need for Black and racialized minority groups to be at the forefront of policing communities and detecting crime, there has been no similar call for a diversity champion to address the even more shocking under-representation of such groups within the education sector. If the agents of law and order require diversity to retain credibility among the communities they serve, then it is curious that the need for such ethnic diversity is ignored when it comes to educating children – or at least Black children. In their submission to the House of Commons Education Committee report on the low educational achievement of poor, White working-class children, the Joseph Rowntree Foundation spoke of a '"middle class ethos" in schools, to which working class children and their parents do not relate', while Diane Reay argued for an education system that 'accords positive value and meaning to working-classness … instead of trying to make [everyone] middle class' (House of Commons Education Committee, 2014: 36). I wonder how often policymakers, academics and government ministers consider what 'positive value and meaning' is given to the cultures, experiences and beliefs of Black working-class children within the middle-class ethos that the Joseph Rowntree Foundation perceptively describes?

In answering that question, I reflect on my own educational journey. School did not even bother to try to make working-class 11-plus failures middle class or afford the slightest positive value and meaning to being Black, female and poor. During my school years, I never saw a Black teacher, nor was I taught about a single Black historian, scientist, inventor or writer. I was presented with a sanitized version of British history where much of the world was waiting to be discovered, civilized and introduced to the benevolence of British Christianity. If I heard anything about Black people, it was in the context of slavery, the Christian mission and British colonialism, where the struggles and sacrifices of my ancestors and the mass slaughter of indigenous peoples were negated in favour of the apparent benefits of British imperialism. I knew little of world history or that there were indigenous people of colour in Australia, New Zealand and the United States long before White settlers colonized their lands. I read no Black literature and assumed that Black people did not act on stage or enjoy music other than soul, gospel, jazz, and rhythm and blues.

Coard (1971) was the first to identify what he saw as endemic racism in British schools and the manner in which Black children were labelled, problematized and alienated from a school system that equated education with a White-normed world view. I came to understand that positive value was primarily ascribed to that which was White and male. Unlike White working-class children whose underachievement is ascribed to their allegedly middle-class schooling alienating them, the schools' attempts to educate me 'White' were not seen as the reason for my own limited academic achievements. Indeed, being 'Black' was the rationale for the teachers' low expectations. I recall being told by my primary school head teacher that 'people like me' would never be anything more than average. When I asked what he meant by 'people like me' the response was 'look in the mirror, I would have thought it was obvious'.

Had my learning been constructed only through the prism of White knowledge I might have grown up thinking that White people discovered everything, invented everything and wrote all of the books worth studying. I might have grown to believe that they practised the only 'proper' religion, symbolized by a male God and a European-looking Jesus born to a White virgin woman. I would have learnt that in order to succeed I had to internalize Whiteness and to be culturally indistinguishable from my White peers. It is what my teachers described as 'integration', but which Coard (1971) saw as part of the cultural bias against Black children, which led to disproportionate numbers being labelled as educationally sub-normal. While I never attracted such a label, I languished for the first two years of secondary school in the bottom stream, with the certain knowledge that I would leave school at 16 and start work.

School and formal lessons were not, however, my only learning nor indeed what had the most lasting impact. I was a small Black girl in a sea of Whiteness. From the age of 7 when I moved from East London to a less urban location, I was an object of curiosity. But, however much I was taught White, I was not White. I was reminded of this simple reality through racial abuse, racial benevolence and liberal paternalism, and by a complete inability to relate myself to any of the teachers or visual images I encountered in school. As I grew up, I came to realize that colour was a defining feature of my humanness to a good number of White people, who exhibited hostile views towards immigrants or anybody they thought looked like one. They saw me as 'other' for reasons that I could not fully comprehend. My colour and physical features defined me either as less than human or as 'the exotic other' – a phenomenon uniquely experienced by Black women who are juxtaposed between racist stereotypes that disparage their womanhood and curiosity about their sexuality and bodies (Collins, 2000). I was exposed to racist insults such as nigger, mongrel and monkey, alongside patronizing attempts to pat my afro hair as if I were a friendly dog grateful for its master's attention. I was also told that I was 'not that Black', even as the same woman was asking if I spoke English.

While individual liberal teachers were reassuring me that 'colour doesn't matter', the hidden curriculum was telling me that it mattered a great deal. It had its roots in slavery, colonialism and imperialism, which had helped to inform attitudes towards Black people and which manifested itself in how I, as a young Black girl, was perceived and the opportunities I would be afforded (Selfa, 2010). When teachers asserted that they treated all children the same, I came to understand that they treated us all as if we were White, and lacked any sensitivity, interest and insight into the realities of a child growing up Black, poor and female in the post-colonial era.

The influence of early schooling and socialization does not stand apart from what is carried into higher education. Swanson and colleagues (2009) report on a number of studies which suggest that, from an early age, African-American children perceive White role models and friendship imagery as preferable to Black. This is similar to David Milner's finding (1975) that children of all colours disproportionately privileged the White doll/image over the Black when asked who they most looked like or would prefer to have as a friend. This suggests that, from an early age, children are not only aware of difference but have also begun to recognize the social value attributed to different skin colours. The psychological and social implications of Black children expressing a preference for Whiteness have neither been taken seriously by policymakers nor have the reasons for the preference been examined.

Spencer (1982) noted that African-American children's preference for White dolls and images did not necessarily mean that such feelings were internalized or associated with their self-concept, noting a difference between young children's racial awareness of the ascribed value of Whiteness, and their personal identity. The numerical presence of African-Americans, their long history of racial struggle and their having as much claim to be called American as White American settlers create a different reality from that of Black people in the UK. In the United States, Black is a political term, directly linked to those of African descent as defined by the Racial Integrity

Act of 1924. In the UK, the term Black has multiple meanings: a descriptor of skin tone, a marker of African heritage, and a broader political term embracing all people not visually White. We are fewer in number, of diverse ethnic origins and, essentially, all migrants or racialized descendants of migrants. This poses additional challenges as to how personal self-esteem is nurtured. Through the school system I gained awareness that Black people were evaluated against White norms and incrementally taught that the backgrounds from which we came were considered at best irrelevant or at worst inferior, and that we ourselves were inferior because of our colour, ethnic origins, gender and class. I, along with others, lived the alienating and identity-destructive reality that Coard (1971) so powerfully described and we suffered accordingly.

Certainly, by the age of 11, I was aware that Whiteness and maleness carried social capital regardless of the person's abilities, effort or human qualities. White was normal, we all knew who was White and I certainly knew that men had more authority and status than women. This normality was reflected in teachers, politicians, policymakers, church leaders and TV stars. It was reflected in toys, books and newspapers and legitimated through biology, religion, history and culture. I did not really question the dominance of Whiteness; it was just the way it was and I was anyway a young, Black female in a society where men had status over women. It was years before I was able to theorize the complex interplay between class, race and gender and the subtle manner in which Black girls and women's tripartite experiences of oppression were silenced and mediated through White women's domination of feminist discourse, White men's dominance of class and Black men's of race epistemology (Crenshaw, 1991). This did not mean that I wanted to be White or male, even while being confused by what it meant to be Black and female. I wanted some of the freedoms and opportunities the boys had and I especially wished that those White people who gave me grief were sufficiently comfortable in their skins not to be threatened by or hostile towards those of a different colour.

Equally, securing self-esteem came at a price and as a means of psychological survival. When you are a child and you see and hear Black people disparaged, when you are exposed to racial taunts and when the core essence of your humanity is questioned by racists, be they ill-informed or intentional, how do you react? How do you respond when you realize that you are only in this country because your ancestors were enslaved and their homelands colonized? What do you say when your classmates are glancing at you as they giggle over pictures of semi-naked indigenous peoples and when a primary school teacher insists on reading *Little Black Sambo* (Bannerman,

1899, this ed. 2007) because 'it's such a lovely story', telling you that it has pictures to which you might relate? As a teenager, what words do you find when you hear people justify discrimination and racial oppression and criticize and condemn those who fought for the freedoms that more socially privileged groups have long enjoyed and take for granted? Where does the confusion and the pain go? How do you belong while you are unable to work out how to belong and gradually realize that you do not, regardless of how integrated and British you might be?

I responded through resistance, becoming tough, hitting the children who insulted me, standing up for other bullied children and being lively and assertive. I became determined to be someone and make something of my life, not for status or money but to confound those who believed that my class, race and gender destined me for mediocrity. For reasons that are still unclear, I was unwilling to accept the ascribed narrative, as I left school with two mediocre O levels but a lifetime of learning and possibilities in front of me. Indeed, despite the fact that Black people say that we have to work twice as hard as White people in order for our contribution to be viewed as equal, I already knew that I was equal – more than equal given what I had already surmounted – to the task of going forward into the adult world, brimming with self-confidence and a passion for human justice.

My journey into the higher education sector cannot be disconnected from the schooling I received and the subliminal messages I absorbed about who I was and what I might go on to be. None of us enters the working world as empty vessels. As Bandura (1977) reminds us, learning is not simply a cognitive process but one that takes place in a social context. We observe people and behaviours, and we see certain behaviours and attitudes reinforced and rewarded, motivating us to act (or not act) accordingly. Bandura's concept of reciprocal determinism is also important in its recognition that people's behaviour influences the environment and that, equally, the environment influences people's behaviour. Black people, White women and the poor experientially knew that truth long before Bandura's theory, since our social advancement has emerged from the struggles, suffering and sacrifices of the oppressed. Trade unions, cooperative and labour movements, gay pride, feminists, womanists, anti-apartheid and civil rights movements have all influenced the social environment and changed attitudes and behaviours accordingly. This understanding became incrementally important to me as I began to better recognize the struggles of oppressed peoples and the racism and sexism against which they fought, and as I journeyed step by step towards a role in higher education.

A career that defined me

How then did a young Black woman from a secondary modern school go on to work as a university academic? The simple answer is that for many years I did not. It was not an aspiration I held or worked towards, and university was not even a word in my vocabulary when I left school at 16. I still consider myself to be an accidental academic and I am not entirely at ease with being one. Having now worked in the higher education sector for 12 years, I am thankful that I was shaped by an earlier career and by different experiences and struggles. Those experiences have enabled me to view higher education institutions dispassionately, to see the challenges faced by Black women academics in a wider social context. I have been exposed to challenges, people, opportunities and understandings that would not have been possible within the Ivory Tower alone. It was in the workplace that my political, racial consciousness both was nurtured and then found expression in activism, and it was during my first career that I came to an increased understanding of racism and the scars, fears and injustice it creates and entrenches. That career was social work.

When I look back, my entry into social work was also pretty accidental. I left school and after a few months of office work I undertook a two-year nursery nursing course with the Children's Society. The course was split between study at what was then Tottenham Technical College and practical experience in a residential nursery in the South East, which looked after babies from 10 days old until they were either adopted or moved to children's homes from aged 5. As I had at school, I found myself caught between two worlds. At college I was the only Black person on my course, but I was surrounded by Black people in the wider college and community – people who embraced me and ensured that I had a great time. It was at college that I was introduced to the subliminal work of Du Bois, specifically his book *The Souls of Black Folk* and his concept of double consciousness:

> It is a peculiar sensation, this double consciousness, this sense of looking at one's self through the eyes of others, of measuring one's soul by the tape of a world that looks on in amused contempt and pity. One ever feels his two-ness—an American, a Negro; two souls, two thoughts, two reconciled strivings; two warring ideals in one dark body, whose dogged strength alone keeps it from being torn asunder.
>
> (Du Bois, 1903: 2–3)

In higher education we often talk of the link between theory and practice and I was able to apply Du Bois' insights to the contradictions in my own life. Being around large numbers of college-based Black people, learning from African-born students about the continent and its struggle to escape the shackles of White colonialism, being drawn to the Pan-African Movement and its role in developing my Black consciousness – little by little I was able to locate my personal experiences within a far broader historical and political context. Audre Lorde's poetry (1978) and the pain and anger that underpinned her early writing spoke to my own struggles, while Angela Davis (1971) expressed such powerful oratory that on reading her book *If They Come in the Morning* I was inspired to grow an afro. Her writings on women, race and class (Davis, 1981) subsequently afforded me new insights into the tripartite nature of my own being. Yet, in those early days, I was submerged in a sea of Whiteness. The other young female students bonded over discussions about boys, hair and make-up, sympathizing over my natural afro hair, encouraging me to get it straightened, and expressing surprise when I refused to do so.

In classes and at the nursery I was being taught a curriculum that seemed to suggest that the only children who existed were White. In the placement setting I was the 'other', yet expected to act and behave as the non-other – as if treating me like I was White meant that I would become White in attitude and values and that my skin colour had no meaning beyond a statement of the obvious. In many ways, this was understandable. Youthful friendships were formed and commonalities shared – none of us exists solely as a colour, unable to find common ground and interests with people of a different hue. Many of my associates saw me as the same as they were. I was being trained alongside them, had been schooled in England and had shared cultural understandings. In the eyes of my White friends, equality was about maintaining such sameness and ignoring my colour. I could not ignore my colour so easily, as it was frequently commented upon and used as a basis for derision, and neither did I wish to. I was, however, an unwitting part of that unspoken conspiracy, quickly learning that those around me felt uncomfortable or antagonistic if I mentioned negative racial experiences or spoke of activities undertaken with Black friends. I therefore adopted the White mask and double consciousness as a strategy for acceptance. I was one of the girls in White company, aware of course of my racial difference but largely keeping its meaning submerged until out with Black friends.

Inevitably, there were individuals who did not treat me as White but who still expected me to behave, relate and think as if I were, despite their discrimination towards me. The more I was encased in a web of Whiteness, the more I became aware of my Blackness and the contradiction during the early part of my career. Despite the nursery being class, White location, 70 per cent of the infants were Black shades and origins. The White babies swiftly moved throug on to same-race adoptive homes, while the majority of the Black children remained, to become damaged by the institutional experience and a lack of love and enduring attachments. At the age of 5 or 6, they were transferred to a residential home in the English countryside, having been at the nursery since they were 10 days old. This situation was especially true for the fair-skinned Black children, in an era when ethnically mixed relationships were unacceptable and the presence of a fair-skinned Black child in a family might suggest such a liaison. The few supposedly lucky Black children who were adopted were usually adopted transracially by well-meaning middle–class, White Christian couples, who genuinely believed that love was always enough. I still wonder about those small children, adults now and perhaps with children of their own. I wonder what sense they made of a care system in which they were the unwanted coloured children and what effect it had on their identity and psychological well-being to grow up in care surrounded by nothing but Whiteness. Were they even double consciousness-aware or do they live out their lives in their Black skins but with their White masks fixed firmly in place?

As a young worker I could not change the system but I could work hard to understand it so that I could ultimately make my own contribution to improving life for those in need. I therefore moved back to inner London and returned to education with a hunger I had not known at school. Alongside evening classes and college-based professional courses I read widely, carved out a Black space where I could debate, argue and learn and open myself up to the wide range of possibilities and insights that education offered. The more I achieved the more I came to realize that academic success was not necessarily linked to intellectual ability or merit but was a manifestation of deeply entrenched class, gender and ethnic inequalities (EHRC, 2010).

By the time I walked into a British university I was a mother and in my twenties. I spent a week at an Open University summer school. I felt intimidated and in awe. I also felt excited and unbelieving that, even for a week, here I was in an institution whose existence I had had no concept of as a child. It was at this summer school that I met the late Professor Stuart Hall, the eminent British-Jamaican sociologist and activist. I was the lone Black participant at the summer school and Professor Hall took time to speak with me and to encourage me, introducing me to some of his work. By the end of the week, I had not only met my first Black academic but also gained insight into a different kind of knowing that enabled me to locate some of my own experiences and emerging understandings within a theoretical context. Hall also introduced me to the work of the French philosopher Michel Foucault (1977, 1980), the link between power and knowledge and the manner in which the former is used to objectivize and define the latter and to exercise social control. During the summer school week, I began to understand that there were differing discourses and tools with which to theorize my lived experiences and gain insights into the social world. It did not especially matter whether I agreed or disagreed with the ideas and concepts expressed. What was important was the exposure to a broad range of theoretical ideas and the opportunity to debate differing perspectives in order to both formulate and challenge my own.

Further and higher education had a role in my developing consciousness, but it remained a sector that I did not think I could or would enter. I was concerned with people and especially people in need or for whom opportunities had been closed or restricted. My increased political, theoretical and social insights merely served to strengthen my values and deepen my resolve to be an advocate against injustice. I spent 20 years living and working alongside some of the most ethnically diverse workforces and communities, and at a time when issues of diversity were being debated, actioned and negated. I learnt so much with and from friends, colleagues and service users as we struggled to understand the individual and structural issues that shaped people's lives and which contributed to injustice. My politics, values, insights and life journey were located within the multiracial communities in which I lived, worked and contributed, and by the many casual and overt forms of racism to which we were subjected.

I can now look back with wry amusement at when, as Assistant Director of Social Services, I was mistaken for a secretary, a cook, and a mother arriving to attend a Black women's group at one of the family centres. I was less amused by the insults, name-calling and marginalization of Black women's contribution and by the manner in which the social capital embedded in White middle-class existence was used as the model against which I was measured, found wanting, and expected to aspire to. I entered a second career in higher education that was not simply moulded by the experience of my work and day-to-day life as a Black woman but approached with an increasingly informed understanding of the political, theoretical, social and economic context in which Black female lives are transacted and experienced.

Transition into higher education

While working as Assistant Director of a London borough, I undertook a part-time MPhil exploring the interconnections between class, race and gender and how that tripartite self was understood and experienced by Black women day-care managers from working-class backgrounds. I had no specific reason for undertaking the study other than a desire to interweave my practice knowledge with continuing intellectual exploration. Interestingly, I undertook the research just after the African-American civil rights activist Kimberlé Crenshaw (1989) introduced the concept of 'intersectionality'. This term theorizes overlapping and interconnecting social identities and their related oppressions. The external examiner (herself a Black woman) encouraged me to publish my findings and, had I done so, I might have made a valued contribution to the unfolding discourse within the UK context. Although I did present a couple of conference papers, I never seriously considered developing the work or making use of the qualification. I did not have the confidence, social capital or contacts to write academically and my experiences at the university had not been entirely positive. There were no Black academics, an all-White peer group and an intellectual disinterest in my work. My career was anyway rooted in social work management and though I enjoyed the research and related reading and study, I completed the MPhil even more convinced that academia was not for people like me.

It was years later that something intellectual stirred and my MPhil was put to use. I had spent some years working as Head of the Children and Families department of a London borough whose children's services were on 'ministerial directions'. This basically meant that the service was so dire and the warnings to improve so numerous that government ministers had intervened. With staffing that was 75 per cent Black and 75 per cent female, my management team and I worked unstintingly to turn around a service that was in chaos, and to support staff teams that were under-resourced and demoralized from years of public criticism and political infighting. Many staff had given committed service to the borough and the children and families they sought to serve. With political support from the newly elected Labour mayor and lead politicians, and with relentless determination, dedication and hard work, the service was inspected four years later and rated as 'serving most people well and with promising prospects', rising from minus nil stars to two of the three then available. Yet those Black staff were never afforded public credit for the improvements to the borough's children's services that they had fought so hard for. That's another story that one day might be told.

After four years I was exhausted not only by the long hours of unremitting and relentless hard work and the complexity of the task, but also by how I was treated as a Black woman senior manager. Although I left with many fantastic memories and enduring friendships after a job collectively well done, I knew that for my physical and mental well-being it was time to move away from senior management in social work. I needed a new challenge and I wanted a better work–life balance. I also wanted some respite from being the successful Black female manager whose temerity in advocating for Black staff and users, and positioning myself within the context of my class, race and gender experiences, rendered me an outsider. The very experiences that gave me the skills, insight, drive and passion to work tirelessly for service improvements in a complex and diverse local authority were still not sufficient, because I was not prepared to keep the White mask firmly in place nor to pretend that racism was a manifestation of Black people's over-sensitive imaginations. Organizations seem to have a problem when we refuse to act as honorary Whites, seek to challenge racism and sexism, and attempt to bring new racial insights to the people we work with and serve. As the title of an Audre Lorde (1984) poem asserts: 'The master's tools will never dismantle the master's house'.

I wanted to continue to contribute to my profession. I felt that my years of experience, my earlier work in training and my accumulated professional credibility might enable me to do so within social work education. I envisaged universities as spaces open to thinking, affording opportunity for differing world views and where academics were not swamped by the micro-management, administration and endless performance targets that had sucked so much time and professional innovation away from local authority practice. (How wrong I was!) Even though I had sound academic and professional qualifications and was at the time the most senior, well-qualified and experienced Black female social work manager in the UK, I did not expect it to be easy securing a post lecturing in social work. My expectations proved to be correct.

I was eventually offered a position in the north of England at a university transitioning from a polytechnic. I certainly did not feel as if I was in the Ivory Tower or even in an academic environment. The course was housed in an overspill building many miles from the main campus and within a city experiencing industrial blight, economic decline and large-scale unemployment. Residents had limited access to higher education and little exposure to people from Black communities. Most students had not been outside the region and spoke of London as if it were a foreign land. The staff were supportive, encouraging and extremely positive about my employment and the experiences I brought. Most did not view themselves as academics in the traditional sense, partly because they had come from social work practice and also because it was an emerging university without a rich research tradition.

Issues within the academy were the least of my problems. Even years later, it is very hard to describe the culture shock of living and working outside London in an area where racism was blatant. During my eight months in the city, I was spat at on the street, called a 'dirty fucking Arab', twice refused service in a shop and spoken to by a core of students as if I were a strange alien who had arrived in their midst. During those months, I was reminded of how alienating it is to live in an environment where there are few other Black people, and to be so visible to those whose own inadequacies make you a target for their fears and derision. The survival strategies I needed to employ to retain my integrity and sense of self were very different from those I used in the multiracial contexts in which I had primarily lived. In those settings, I had numerous Black friends and colleagues; White colleagues were largely comfortable with cosmopolitan London and had chosen to work in diverse London boroughs. My induction to higher education was therefore a sharp learning curve and it was with a sense of utter relief that, after nine months in the job, I packed up my rented flat and headed out of the city for the last time.

I spent a further 11 years at three different universities: two post-1990 modern universities with a large percentage of Black and minority ethnic students, and a post-1960 university with a less socially and ethnically diverse student body. I have also completed doctoral study at a high-performing post-1960 university. I went into higher education generally subscribing to Muhammad Ali's view that 'I know where I'm going and I know the truth, and I don't have to be what you want me to be. I'm free to be what I want' (Lipsyte, 1964). Such freedom is, however, an illusion because what we want to be is mediated by the expectations and behaviour of others and not simply by our own knowledge and intentions.

A number of colleagues at the two modern universities have been positive advocates of equality and supportive peers. They remain largely rooted in the founding values that underpin the social work profession, and their teaching and placement contact with a large and socially diverse group of students and practitioners ensure a balance between academia and the practice needs of students and the profession. Very few come from traditional academic backgrounds, having had careers of varying lengths away from academia and, like myself, largely drawn to universities as contributors to social work education and training, rather than through a desire to be academics per se. It is also perhaps more difficult to acquire delusions of grandeur in the modern universities, given that their research profiles are more limited, their academic status less assured and their student intakes educationally and socially diverse. While the absence of Black peers is personally isolating, there are sufficient commonalities and shared commitments to make the day-to-day experience racially manageable. Additionally, I am no longer seeking to establish myself and I have never cared for the glitter balls that might be dangled before me as a reward for conformity.

The post-1960 university where I worked for five years was a culture shock of a different kind. I had been used to working as part of a corporate organization and where service improvements and effective practice could not be secured through individual endeavours alone. I was also used to working with staff who often put aside personal aspiration to do their best for the communities they served. Not only did I have to adjust to never seeing a Black or Brown face within the academy, but I also had to adjust to the individualistic people whose primary motivation appeared to be their own careers. The module approach to teaching, the concept of academic freedom and the need for academics to compete for research funding seemingly mitigate against the concept of 'team'. A culture of garden parties, gown and town parades and insider language is alien to those of us from working-class backgrounds and appears to embed an elitism that reinforces that sense of alienation. This is not simply a class issue, although class clearly permeates higher education, but also one of race and gender and the cumulative educational impact of all three (Reay *et al.*, 2005).

For those wedded to academia it can perhaps be easy to assume that the only real knowledge is that garnered through publications and formal research. Practice expertise is afforded a far lower status than academic learning and published research; people's lived experiences can easily be dismissed if they cannot be proven as valid through formal studies or theorized into books. If experience can be thus devalued, then so too can those who live and articulate the experience. My long and successful career of direct relevance to the course on which I worked counted for little, as did the knowledge and insights I brought as a Black woman. At the time, I did not have 'Dr' before my name, I had not published in influential journals and had no respected research tradition. Any real or perceived challenges regarding race – and how well students were being prepared for the socially and ethnically diverse profession they were to enter – were largely unwelcome and, in the eyes of some colleagues, expressed only by a troublesome academic nobody, cast adrift in a sea of Whiteness and very important somebodies. Given that I had a life and an identity away from the university, that reaction might have been manageable, were it not for the Black students who approached me about their negative experiences in the university and on placement, the negation of their cultural knowledge, and the allegedly racist comments from a few fellow students and practitioners. They expected that I, as a Black person, would not only understand, but would also speak out. Speaking out was something that I had, with difficulty, learnt to do. As Audre Lorde's poem 'A litany for survival' reminds us:

> and when we speak we are afraid
> our words will not be heard
> nor welcomed
> but when we are silent
> we are still afraid
>
> So it is better to speak
> remembering
> we were never meant to survive

(Lorde, 1978)

Speaking out on behalf of the students was painful when the exposure of students' unfair treatment was not addressed and my intervention was resented; not least from those who spoke out and expected to be heard when it came to inequalities that affected White women and men. The cost of speaking out against unfair employment practices that sought to hand out a year-long contract with no open competition led to criticism and isolation. Speaking out about racism led to accusations of bullying. As the person speaking out, I became the one problematized along with the student, rather than the racist behaviour. As with so many manifestations of racism and sexism, such actions could not be proven to the satisfaction of those academics who were isolated from the struggles of Black people, had little exposure to their lives and experiences, and who were given little incentive to change. After all, what is the point of an Ivory Tower if you are not undisturbed within its turrets?

The dominant White narrative thus prevailed; a narrative framed, I would argue, by fear and guilt. Lorde (1984) suggests that guilt is a response to one's own actions or non-actions; a response that frequently masks defensiveness, impotence and the protection of one's ignorance. I had to re-evaluate many of the gender and racial assumptions I had previously acquired. It was not that former work settings were an oasis of racial and gender tranquillity or that sexism, racism or inter-Black differences did not feature. They most certainly did, but they were live issues, existing as part of the broader management and practice script of how services were delivered to people in need and what it meant to be part of and manage within a multiracial team. Over the years it had been possible to secure equality change through collective hard work and sheer determination. The critical mass of Black people and the challenges faced by poor inner-city communities meant that racism, sexism and Islamophobia could not just be ignored. Practices were in place to deal with the worst manifestations of racism and sexism, and there were enough individuals to provide a variety of perspectives and to take action where needed.

Universities in contrast are communities within themselves, privileged by tradition and framed by a historical context of elitism and social advantage. My experiences suggest that they appear to operate by their own codes; temporary or permanent contracts are not always subject to open recruitment, doctorates and teaching qualifications are required for some positions while staff in the same subject area who have neither can be on an identical job title or higher salary grade. The criteria for promotion are largely framed by the amount of research money secured or publications of international impact. Hourly-paid lecturers are frequently recruited on the basis of who you (and they) know, with various excuses offered as to why such opportunities cannot be externally advertised against transparent criteria. These seemingly entrenched practices make the sector far less penetrable by potential staff from less traditional academic backgrounds or educational traditions, including, but not exclusively, Black people.

In addition, there is no apparent incentive to address the ethnic profile of staff or doctoral students in a culture driven primarily by the targets that contribute to league table status or funding success. When questions are asked about the number of Black academics there is tendency to lump together both internationally recruited academics and 'home' staff, regardless of the Black and racialized groups from which they originate. This approach masks the inequalities that exist between different ethnic groups and subverts challenges from Black academics as to why they are under-represented. The subtle and overt ways in which advantage is entrenched within higher education are explored in Singh and Kwhali (2015). Black and racialized minorities enter a sector historically founded upon academic elitism that grants entry to a privileged minority by excluding the less privileged majority. Epistemology has become interwoven with the voices and narratives of the dominant, whose inability to stand outside that privilege is equal only to their resentment of any challenge to it.

If the higher education system has no evident strategy for addressing the under-representation of British Black academics, then the chances of

UK universities using the narratives and experiences of Black academics to contribute to the formulation of knowledge and truth are even more remote. At best, such institutional indifference promotes a deficit approach to Black people that focuses on our apparent need for mentoring and special training courses in order to progress, and at worst it reflects an attitude of racial indifference or an implicit assumption that academic appointments are made solely on the basis of merit – of which White people apparently have more. Hence the concept of private troubles can be turned around to promote the idea that private success is down to individual effort, open to anybody who works hard and that such success is itself evidence of a structural and organizational commitment to gender and racial equality.

Conclusion

In many ways I feel privileged to have spent time in higher education. It has been a privilege to contribute to the dreams of individual students and support them in their studies, to have the opportunity to read and research and to know that my presence has, in some small way, made a difference to countless students and some current and former colleagues. I have worked outside the academy long enough to know how hard working life is for so many people and that their intellect, potential, energy and passion can be crushed by the relentless toil and routine nature of so many jobs. I am aware that my role and qualifications afford me opportunities of which thousands of other Black women are equally deserving. Equally, my illusion of higher education has been shattered. I have experienced within its walls an intellectual and class arrogance that privileges academic status above all else and negates the intellectual contribution and interests of Black and minority ethnic staff. I have experienced institutional indifference to the paucity of Black academics and the consequent wasted talent. I have seen minority students pay fees in increasing numbers to universities that promote their commitment to diversity while exposing students to European insights and understandings, delivered by all-White academic teams.

While privileged, I am not grateful. I have been given nothing other than a job, and in each university the same job, so I have little need to feel gratitude given that I acquired the skills for the job outside the academy rather than within it. I have given back in hours, commitment and contribution more than I have taken. None of the institutions at which I have worked has attempted to understand how racial aloneness is experienced or how the knowledge that arises from my gender and race co-exists alongside the need to satisfy the White criteria of meaning. It is Black friendships and my own tenacity that kept me afloat within a higher education institution that would gladly have left me to drown.

Ultimately, I only have my story. I cannot know what it is to be another colour or gender than I am, or to experience being born in a different place, social context or time. I cannot travel another journey or claim insider knowledge of organizations and universities of which I have not been a part. Yet, I also know that my story will find resonance in the stories of sisters and brothers of different skin shades, ages and genders. That is because my story is also their story in its context if not in its detail. I can tell my story because I stand on the shoulders of generations of Black people who have sacrificed their lives, freedoms and opportunities to secure the advancements I now enjoy. I can tell my story because Black people have written books, poems and music that have spoken to my soul and to my understandings. I have been affirmed and encouraged by Black sisters and brothers who have shared the pain of racism and sexism and shared the joy and hope of racial progress.

I do not need to be in a specific university to know that there are other Black women striving to be whole and enacting strategies for survival – some of which will be harmful to their human dignity and detrimental to the memories of those who struggled before us. They too are sisters, in a society whose racism and sexism they did not create. I can tell my story as I have come to understand that knowledge is not the preserve of Europeans and that the knowledge of my formal education was designed to silence me – to have me believe that I was nothing unless I defined success through White prisms of meaning and intellectual thought. It is not, however, the telling of the story that is important – it is the learning, the struggle, the hurt, the experiences, the politicizing and theorizing of that story that take the narrative to something more than a set of words.

When I began to work in higher education, I believed it to be something that it is not. I carried into the academy the poverty of my youth, a working life and the ongoing challenge of integrating into White organizational systems while being free to give active expression to my race, class and gender identity. The years of experience and struggle, of slights and insults and of Black friendships and shared endeavours, were a part of who I was and who I continue to be. I am, in large part, what this society has created, and that includes the racism and sexism that have shaped my personal evolution. Hence, I have never been and will never truly be an 'academic'. I am a Black woman from a working-class background who made good in order to give something back to the Black elders, writers, colleagues, friends and ancestors whose love and survival have made my journey possible. I made good to confound those who thought I was destined to 'make bad' and because I believe that we are on this earth to serve others. I have had to construct meaning through race and gender and come to a love of myself as a fair-skinned Black woman while knowing that the story is not about race and gender in isolation. Racial progress has been advanced alongside Black men who are our brothers, fathers, lovers and friends, and whose lives, experiences and destinies cannot be separated from our own. There have also been many honourable and committed White people who are part of my life script and who have held out their hands in friendship and love. Even the racists, the ignorant, the bullies and the indifferent are victims of their nation's racial legacy and of their own fear and guilt.

There will be other Black women who will follow me; some whose lives will be shaped by economic, educational and social advantage and some who will have to fight harder to gain educational qualifications, employment opportunities and self-respect. I hope they are able to draw from the rich history of Black knowledge, tenacity and experience, and to know they can aspire to human completeness by loving themselves and other Black people in order to be valued and whole. They do not need to be that which they are not, or to be grateful for the crumbs from the White man's table. I also know that some such women will have the strength to challenge injustice, to speak out against racism and misogyny and to retain a vision of higher education that truly embraces the rich world history that has shaped us all. I know that there will be others who will aspire to little more than making it and achieving a certain job title or award, indifferent to those who walked before, who pull up the ladder on those they could potentially lift. What I do know is that both within and outside the academy, Black voices will never be silenced, our different and interlinking stories will be told and injustices will be challenged. History teaches me that – even though I did not learn such history in the Ivory Tower!

References

Bandura, A. (1977) *Social Learning Theory*. Englewood Cliffs, NJ: Prentice Hall.

Bannerman, H. (2007) *The Story of Little Black Sambo*. Minneapolis: Filiquarian Publishing.

Coard, B. (1971) *How the West Indian Child Is Made Educationally Sub-Normal in the British School System: The scandal of the black child in schools in Britain*. London: New Beacon Books.

Collins, P.H. (2000) *Black Feminist Thought: Knowledge, consciousness, and the politics of empowerment*. 2nd ed. New York: Routledge.

Crenshaw, K. (1989) 'Demarginalizing the intersection of race and sex: A black feminist critique of antidiscrimination doctrine, feminist theory and antiracist politics'. *University of Chicago Legal Forum*, 139–67.

— (1991) 'Mapping the margins: Intersectionality, identity politics, and violence against women of color'. *Stanford Law Review*, 43, 1241–99.

Davis, A.Y. (1971) *If They Come in the Morning: Voices of resistance*. New York: Third Press.

— (1981) *Women, Race and Class*. New York: Random House.

Du Bois, W.E.B. (1903) *The Souls of Black Folk*. Chicago: A.C. McClurg and Co.

EHRC (Equality and Human Rights Commission) (2010) *How Fair is Britain? Equality, human rights and good relations in 2010: The first triennial review.* Manchester: EHRC. Online. www.equalityhumanrights.com/sites/default/files/how_fair_is_britain_-_complete_report.pdf (accessed 1 February 2017).

Fanon, F. (1986) *Black Skin, White Masks*. London: Pluto Press.

Foucault, M. (1977) *Discipline and Punish: The birth of the prison*. Trans. Sheridan, A. London: Allen Lane.

— (1980) *Power/Knowledge: Selected interviews and other writings, 1972–1977*. Ed. and trans. Gordon, C. Brighton: Harvester Press.

House of Commons Education Committee (2014) *Underachievement in Education by White Working Class Children*. London: The Stationery Office.

House of Commons Home Affairs Committee (2016) *Police Diversity*. London: House of Commons.

Lipsyte, R. (1964) 'Clay Discusses His Future, Liston and Black Muslims'. *New York Times*, 27 February. Online. www.nytimes.com/books/98/10/25/specials/ali-future.html (accessed 17 October 2017).

Lorde, A. (1978) *The Black Unicorn*. New York: W.W. Norton and Company.

— (1984) 'The master's tools will never dismantle the master's house'. In Lorde, A. *Sister Outsider: Essays and speeches*. Freedom, CA: Crossing Press.

Milner, D. (1975) *Children and Race*. London: Penguin Books.

Reay, D., David, M.E. and Ball, S. (2005) *Degrees of Choice: Class, race, gender and higher education*. Stoke-on-Trent: Trentham Books.

Selfa, L. (2010) 'The roots of racism'. *Socialist Worker*, 21 October. Online. https://socialistworker.org/2010/10/21/the-roots-of-racism (accessed 1 March 2017).

Singh, G. and Kwhali, J. (2015) *How Can We Make Not Break Black and Minority Ethnic Leaders in Higher Education?* (Stimulus Paper). London: Leadership Foundation for Higher Education.

Spencer, M.B. (1982) 'Personal and group identity of Black children: An alternative synthesis'. *Genetic Psychology Monographs*, 106 (1), 59–84.

Swanson, D.P., Cunningham, M., Youngblood, J. and Spencer, M.B. (2009) 'Racial identity development during childhood'. *GSE Publications*, 198. Online. http://repository.upenn.edu/cgi/viewcontent.cgi?article=1203&context=gse_pubs (accessed 29 July 2017).

Chapter 2

Overcoming objectification and dehumanization in academia

Deborah Gabriel

> *Domination always involves the objectification of the dominated.*
> (Maynard, cited in Collins, 1986: S18)

Introduction

This chapter is a critical reflection on and analysis of what it is to be objectified and dehumanized as a Black female academic. Objectification and dehumanization as the 'other' is a typical component of Black women's raced and gendered experiences (Collins, 1986, 1989). Through critical reflective analysis I seek to highlight the role played by objectification and dehumanization in maintaining our status as 'others' and keeping us on the periphery of academic life. Using Black feminist theory as a critical lens helps me to make sense of my experiences through a unique standpoint, of and for Black women, that involves self-definition and self-valuation as tools of resistance (Collins, 1989). In this chapter, I also highlight the role that community networking and sister relationships have played in supporting my survival and progress within academia.

Objectification and dehumanization

Objectification is defined as treating people like objects, while dehumanization refers to seeing and treating people as if they are not human (Gervais *et al.*, 2013). Dehumanization can involve the denial of human attributes to groups or individuals (ibid.) as is the case with people of African descent, or those of us racialized as Black. Throughout history, Black people have been subjected to objectification and dehumanization, with many of the ideologies that underpinned our systemized dehumanization during European slavery being espoused during the Enlightenment by celebrated White philosophers. For example, in his *Lectures on the Philosophy of World History (1822–8)*, Georg Hegel proposed that Africans remain in a perpetual child-like state of being where they have no consciousness of their existence as human beings

(Eze, 1997). In 1775, in his essay *On National Characteristics, So Far as They Depend Upon the Distinct Feeling of the Sublime*, Immanuel Kant suggested that Africans are incapable of moral and aesthetic feeling (ibid.). Kant regarded objectification as the denial of humanity, which results in objectified people being perceived as existing purely to serve the ends of others (Loughnan *et al.*, 2010). The sexual objectification of Black women was most pronounced during European slavery, when the rape of Black female slaves was legitimized through their interlinked status as chattel and concubine (Jordan, 1962) and through their construction and representation as hyper-sexual, amoral beings – the antithesis of White female virtue (Craig, 2006). The present-day dehumanization and objectification of Black people should therefore be regarded as legacies of White European slavery and colonization, rooted in White supremacy.

When I was undertaking my PhD in media and cultural studies from 2010 to 2014, I taught on undergraduate degree courses in journalism. During my first year, I became the object of racist and sexist discourse exchanged between a group of White students on Facebook, three of whom were women. Their online conversation, during which they referred to me by my race and gender in animalistic and graphic sexual terms, took place during my class, where they laughed openly, though at the time I was unaware I was the brunt of their jokes. While their actions enraged me, I also felt a profound sense of disappointment – not least because I had willingly gone to great lengths to support some of those very students when they had come to me for additional assistance with their work. Their behaviour demonstrated not just a profound lack of respect for me as their tutor, but also spoke to their rejection of me as a human being worthy of respect. Racist and sexist ideologies are often expressed in animalistic terms (Collins, 1986), where controlling images of Black women help to normalize racism and emphasize our outsider status. It is a way of signifying our un-belonging (Collins, 1990).

A key reason why we, as Black women, are frequently objectified as the 'other' is because we do not conform to the dominant, normative conception of an academic, which is a status reserved for White men primarily, but also for White women. The term 'space invaders' describes the status of Black women as outsiders in British academia occupying a White, male-dominated space (Puwar, 2004), where marginalization, over-scrutinizing and the absence of a sense of belonging characterize our experience (Wright *et al.*, 2007). Space invaders is an apt definition, since it is argued that we do not embody that which is deemed 'normal' or 'natural' and, in this regard, are perceived as alien others, since 'the White male body is taken as the norm' (ibid.: 149).

The experience of being over-scrutinized in academia is not limited to staff, since there is also a tendency among students to question the credibility of Black academics. Discrimination is sometimes projected through negative comments on course feedback that are often personalized (Bhopal and Jackson, 2013). During my academic life, students have made personalized comments in course feedback at several of the universities at which I have taught. On one occasion, I was unfavourably compared with a White, female colleague, with whom I taught the same course and whose style of teaching is similar to my own. But I was not evaluated in the same way, since 'Black bodies entering spaces not traditionally reserved for them are in a tenuous position' (Wright *et al.*, 2007: 149). I have come to believe that, just as during European slavery Black women were constructed as the antithesis of White females, so women academics of colour are perceived to be the opposite of our White female colleagues and therefore seen as 'out of place' (ibid.). Dominant, Western ideologies racialize Black people in oppositional terms, not merely as different, and objectification is a key part of this process (Collins, 1990). Being objectified means being defined, labelled and positioned by others, and thereby subordinated.

My PhD thesis focused on Black bloggers in the UK, examining their motivation, gratification and use of blogs as discursive activism. Most of the participants were women, many of whom shared their experiences of raced and gendered discrimination:

> There was that whole thing about the lecturer who said that Black women weren't attractive. I was pissed off about that and … it really got me thinking, you know, how we are seen. We are either demonised or fantasied, it's one extreme to the other.
>
> (Chioma, cited in Gabriel, 2014: 129)

My doctoral thesis drew theoretically and conceptually on Black feminism and critical race theory. I found that analysing the experiences of the participants, which bore similarities to my own biography, helped me to better understand my raced and gendered experiences in academia. It highlighted how Black women speak up and speak out as a response to being objectified and dehumanized in the media and popular culture, and demonstrated the importance of creating spaces to enhance our voice and visibility and to counter marginalization and exclusion.

Ironically, while invisibility is a key dimension of our experiences as Black women in higher education, hyper-visibility is equally problematic.

not fit the normative identity of an academic but, as Ahmed (2009) we are the embodiment of diversity. Our presence symbolizes visual often taken as a sign of progress, since diversity is frequently approached through higher education policy as a numbers game, where the aim is to add colour to the sea of White faces. Such approaches promote a conceptualization of Black people as additives to the existing structures and systems, which means that the institutional culture – which is the problem – remains unchanged while we get added to a system that was not created for us. Since we are accommodated into a White system, we are supposed to be grateful and therefore come under pressure not to talk about racism. As others occupying spaces in someone else's system, 'it is this very structural position of being the guest or the stranger, the one who received hospitality, which keeps us in certain places' (Ahmed, 2009: 42). It is for this reason that Ahmed calls on us to 'reclaim the figure of the angry Black feminist' (ibid.: 41).

Talking back

My isolation as a PhD student at a Northern university, hundreds of miles away from family and friends in London and the South, increased my sense of vulnerability, as did the racism and sexism I experienced there. This motivated me to establish Black British Academics in 2013, with the aim of creating a community: a critical mass to give us voice and visibility. My aims were to highlight the value of our intellectual and cultural capital and our contribution to the knowledge economy. The findings of my PhD thesis highlighted that building intellectual and cultural capital is something Black people do very well, though it goes unnoticed and unacknowledged. I was frustrated by the lack of attention paid to race equality in higher education and felt that people of colour should be defining and leading on strategies and initiatives. Ahmed (2007) argues that, in recent years, equality and diversity documents are imbued with a performative quality, in that they are frequently regarded as delivering equality simply by expressing commitment, with little monitoring of whether the equality measures are put into practice. In marketing materials, higher education institutions frequently make reference to 'valuing diversity', usually accompanied by images of ethnically diverse students implying that diversity already exists within the organization. However, the absence of either a strong economic or moral association means the emphasis on diversity is merely about difference as opposed to justice, and therefore lacking any substance in terms of addressing racial inequalities. Other critics make similar arguments – that the diversity agenda acknowledges difference rather than highlighting the discrimination people experience on the basis of race, class, gender, age and other characteristics (Jones, 2006). Writing equality policies is insufficient to engender institutional change – to do that, policies must be put into practice (Ziegert and Hanges, 2005).

The academy is a space where colour-blind ideologies, which normalize the dominance of Whites in society while obscuring processes of racism and racialization, are developed, maintained, reinforced and embedded in curricula, policies and practices (Leonardo, 2004). The starting point for understanding racial oppression should be critical analyses of the experiences of people of colour (ibid.). Sharing our experiences as Black women in academia provides significant experiential knowledge to generate understandings on the dynamics of race, ethnicity, culture and gender and how they influence structural power relations. 'Talking back' in a Black feminist context means speaking in a compelling way to make our voices heard and not just listened to (hooks, 1989).

During 2013, the year I established Black British Academics, I wrote a series of articles about the experiences of Black academics in the UK, that were published in *The Independent* and *The Guardian*: 'Self-empowerment is the best way to defeat racism in academia' (Gabriel, 2013a), 'Ethnic and gender inequalities in postgraduate study still aren't being addressed' (Gabriel, 2013b), 'Race equality in academia: Time to establish Black studies in the UK?' (Gabriel, 2013c) and 'Race equality in academia: We've got a huge way to go' (Gabriel, 2013d). My aim was to 'talk back', to tell it how it is – how racism manifests in higher education and why it persists. Ironically, my first article written for *The Independent* came about because I 'talked back' in response to an article by another writer about Black academics, which I was interviewed for, but which was headed by a photo of Cornel West. 'I admire Cornel West,' I told the editor, 'but he's an African-American – the story is about Black British academics – this is just another way to make us invisible.' The editor understood where I was coming from, changed the photo to one I supplied and invited me to write a piece to give our perspective. It's great when you talk back and people listen.

There are few occasions that inspire me to talk back in a way that truly expresses anger and resentment, as Ahmed advocates (2009). However, one such incident occurred during July 2016 when I met one of my former students in London. She had recently graduated and I was immensely proud of her for her dissertation on the cultural appropriation of Black women's bodies from a Black feminist perspective. She soon became visibly angry and distressed as she recounted her experience of objectification and dehumanization when a White student wore blackface at the university summer ball and refused to remove it when she asked him to. Her plea fell on deaf ears – the blackened ears of the offending student but also the ears of university staff and a campus policeman who were present. My anger increased when she showed me a picture of the student on her phone – then all at once I saw an opportunity to talk back and to make her voice heard this time; to make my voice heard by the university leadership, and to make the voices of Black students heard, students who are routinely dehumanized in their everyday experiences within a Eurocentric environment. I felt I had a moral obligation to speak and adopted resistance poetry as the mode of address with 'In critique of blackface and institutional resistance to racism' (Gabriel, 2016a). I felt like the proud 'Angry Black Woman' talking back 'without a hint of regret' that Rachel Alicia Griffin (2012: 140) unleashes in her autoethnography, as the words 'Neanderthal', 'imbecile' and 'fool' rolled off my lips as I typed them into the computer. I published the article on the Black British Academics' website and across social media. Colleagues I passed in the corridor would tell me how much they enjoyed my poem, and it formed the basis of alliances within the institution that are helping to chip away at the Whiteness within our university. As Black women, we may be 'disciplined' (ibid.: 39) not to talk back, but sometimes talking back is necessary.

Raced and gendered oppression by White women in the academy

> Of white feminists we must ask, what exactly do you mean when you say we?
>
> (Carby, 1996: 52)

Hazel Carby posed this question in her provocative chapter entitled 'White women listen! Black feminism and the boundaries of sisterhood'. She explained succinctly why the needs and interests of Black women should not be an afterthought or additive to a Eurocentric White female agenda. That, over ten years later, we are still having to call out White women for marginalizing and excluding us from gender equality spaces in academia is the biggest reason why we must continue to talk back as Black women. The occasions on which I have felt most compelled to talk back as the Angry Black Woman have been when approached by White women who subscribe to Emmanuel Kant's notion that people are objectified to serve the interests of others, in this case that Black women exist to serve the interests of White women. A few months ago, two White female academics who were guest-editing the special issue of a journal focused on gender and intersectionality asked if I would review an article on gender issues in Uganda. My first feeling was that I had been asked as an afterthought, purely because of their likely inability to relate to gender issues outside their own Euro-centred context, as opposed to the editors involving women of colour from the outset in the editorial process. I was not impressed. But on reading the call for papers I became incensed because, despite the inclusion of the term 'intersectionality', there was no reference to raced and gendered experiences other than that of White women and the tokenistic theme 'gender and multi-ethnic families'. Part of my response to them was:

> I am disappointed that your call for papers that you attached demonstrates the exclusionary Whiteness which I so often find among gender scholars. There is little in your call that engages with raced and gendered experiences despite the fact that you have appropriated the term 'intersectionality' developed by the Black feminist scholar and critical race theorist, Professor Kimberlé Crenshaw. How dare you appropriate the intellectual capital of Black women and then use it outside its original context and meaning, erasing us in the process? It incenses me when we, as women of colour, are marginalised and de-valued in this way.

Black feminist scholar Nikol Alexander-Floyd (2012) argues that Crenshaw's seminal work, which was intended to draw attention to the limitations of (White) feminism, has been appropriated in a manner that subjugates Black women's knowledge. To be fair, some White feminist scholars have also critiqued such use. Sirma Bilge (2013: 405) defines such appropriation as 'whitening intersectionality', and that it forms part of a neoliberal agenda and has a depoliticizing impact on Black feminist construction of intersectional experiences. Anna Carastathis (2014: 304) asserts that the appropriation of intersectionality within White-dominated feminist discourses serves to 'obscure its origins in Black feminist thought'. Black feminism has always been a politically oriented mission, whereas the appropriation of intersectionality by some feminist scholars reduces it to a fanciful term in academic writing without even acknowledging its origins.

If such experiences – of being asked to serve the needs of White women and further enhance their privilege – were rare, it would not be so bad, but they have become almost routine. Just last month, a White female academic contacted me to ask if I 'or someone' in Black British Academics would sign a letter of protest at the exclusion of women from a major event in the North. The letter read: 'Only 13% (13/98) speakers were female and press releases uncovered "all male panels"'. 'What consultation will occur

in advance of 2018 to ensure diverse representation including ethnicities/
disabilities?' I was again incensed and offered a swift reply:

> Having read the letter it appears that the concern of the signatories
> lies purely with the gender imbalance – there is nothing other than
> a cursory mention of racial exclusion in the second paragraph
> where people of colour are not even referred to as people but
> lumped together with disabled people: 'ethnicities/disabilities'.
>
> This really says a lot. That if you are White you are valued as a
> person and can be referred to as 'female' and 'women' but if you
> happen to be a person of colour you are marginalised and merely
> an afterthought in the quest for (White) female equality. I wonder
> how many of the 98 speakers were non-White or how many of
> the signatories actually care.
>
> Black British Academics was not established to fight equality
> battles for White women who never consider women of colour in
> their quest to be on an equal footing with men and who have no
> real interest in race equality or stop to think for a moment about
> their own White privilege.

So, like Hazel Carby (1996: 52), I must also ask of White feminists 'what
exactly do you mean when you say we?'

The role of allies in the struggle for equality

In classes I have taught where the topic of discrimination has surfaced, I say
to students: 'You don't have to be a person of colour to speak out against
racism.' I do this to create inclusion around race equality issues and a sense
of responsibility, advocating that 'we should all speak up against all forms
of discrimination'. That some White students and staff routinely fail to
see the ways in which Black women, and people of colour generally, are
discriminated against through everyday practice is further evidence of just
how normalized our dehumanized status is. Whiteness is a word that rarely
crosses the lips of the dominant group in academia because they never
stop to reflect or think about their White privilege or the ways in which
they benefit from it, yet it would be extremely valuable 'to self-reflectively
examine how White racism works' (Scheurich, 1993: 5). I have often been
in conversations with White colleagues (within and outside my institution)
where I have shared an experience of racism and the response is a look of
sympathetic bewilderment. Students, too, seldom have a consciousness of
White privilege as an active process that confers disadvantage on people

of colour because 'their textbooks reinforce the innocence of Whiteness' (Leonardo, 2004: 138). In order to transform the institutional culture within academia to one that is culturally democratic and equitable, White students and staff need to become active participants in challenging Whiteness. I agree with Scheurich, a White scholar, that the starting point for addressing racism is to acknowledge that everyone is affected in significant ways by their membership of a racial group:

> Whites need to study and report how being White affects our thinking, our behaviours, our attitudes and our decisions from the micro personal level to the macro social level ... All Whites are socially positioned as Whites and receive social advantages because of this positionality. No individual White gets to be an exception because of his or her antiracism.
>
> (Scheurich, 1993: 9)

Career development and progression

At my interview in July 2014 for a post as a lecturer at Bournemouth University, I spoke proudly of being the founder of Black British Academics and about its contribution to the higher education sector. When I subsequently joined the institution, the acting head of department ensured that Black British Academics was included in my workload plan, as professional practice. It has profoundly shaped the three key areas of my academic role: in teaching, research and professional practice. I attribute my promotion in 2016 to senior lecturer to my association with Black British Academics, as I argued in a post I wrote for my blog: 'Another year in the life of an early career researcher' (Gabriel, 2016b).

My key contributions to teaching have involved the innovation of pedagogies of social justice and cultural democracy as an approach to diversifying the curriculum and transforming the institutional culture. This originated from consultancy work with Aisha Richards at the University of the Arts London undertaken through Black British Academics through the programme she pioneered called 'Shades of Noir'. This inspired me to develop a new final-year degree option called Media Inequality, which aimed to enhance the representation of people of colour in the communication industries. These contributions to teaching helped me to gain fellowship of the Higher Education Academy and I am now involved in mentoring staff through our internal scheme and in assessing applications as a panel member. I have recently won two internal awards connected with curriculum diversification through social justice pedagogy to extend its implementation across the institution and develop a research impact case study. Some of my research has been devoted to examining the dynamics of race, ethnicity and culture in higher education.

This book is one such project, initially developed through Black Sister Network – a dedicated space within Black British Academics for women of colour. Another forthcoming book project with Trentham emerged from the PhD Network within Black British Academics, co-authored with Professor Kevin Hylton: *A Sense of Belonging: Race, ethnicity and culture in higher education*. In addition, I have been offered external opportunities with mention of Black British Academics in the invitation, such as editorial board and chairing positions, as well as guest and keynote lectures. In my blog post I assert that, while my institution has introduced positive measures, offering accessibility to staff development and transparency in the promotion process through independent pay and promotion panels, such initiatives can sometimes be undermined by cliques at faculty and departmental level, where the roles and opportunities that contribute to meeting the criteria for promotion to a higher grade are not always made available to everyone. While cliques often form through gender and class associations, I have felt isolated at times, because of my critical focus on race in my research and teaching practice.

Thomas and colleagues (1999) argue that marginalization and isolation of Black academics are partially attributable to the divergence between dominant, traditional approaches to subject areas and research, and our aims of integrating a social justice focus linked to our experiences as racialized minorities. Approaches that seek to expose and challenge the centrality of Whiteness are often relegated in favour of mainstream, dominant world views. Despite this reality, I feel that race, ethnicity and culture have played a significant role in my career progression thus far, as my quest has imbued me with a political identity, strength and voice – an experience I share with other Black women. Alfred (2001: 123) argues that, within institutional cultures premised on White, male hegemony (and I would add to that White female hegemony), Black women develop bicultural competence by accessing their 'bicultural life structure'. This is defined as 'the nucleus from which people of colour evoke the power to contest the terrain of differences that contribute to their marginal positions in White-dominated organisations' (ibid.). The ongoing struggle against White hegemony within academia promotes agency, through which we, as Black women, develop successful strategies for navigating culturally dominant organizational environments. The integration of Black British Academics into my role as an academic creates synergy between the key dimensions of my role. This has created opportunities for collaboration and collective activism both within Black British Academics and in the wider community of staff and students in higher education committed to racial equality. Collectively, we resist the dominance and centrality of Whiteness that exists in academia as an active process of self-determination and participation in self-empowerment (Karenga, 1980).

The value of community and sister relationships

Black feminist thought reflects a positionality by and for Black women, of which self-definition and self-valuation are key themes (Collins, 1990). The former involves challenging external, stereotypical constructions of Black womanhood and the latter involves replacing such constructions with 'authentic Black female images' (Collins, 1986: S17). Dominant, stereotypical constructions form part of the dehumanizing process that contributes to the exploitation of Black women and is a mechanism for suppressing our resistance. Self-definition is an important component of self-empowerment, since it is not merely about challenging what is said about us as Black women but of challenging the act of others defining us. In defining ourselves as Black women we promote self-empowerment by reclaiming our humanity, which is a form of activism in itself (ibid.).

In the acknowledgements page of my PhD thesis, I express admiration for participants in my study, who are also members of an online community that I had set up, called Black Bloggers UK and International Network, before embarking on my research. I dedicate my thesis to my siblings, my late parents and my late grandmother and thank my sister friends for their encouragement and support. They have all played an important role in defining who I am and helping me to develop and retain a critical consciousness: 'the "inside" ideas that allow Black women to cope with and, in most cases, transcend the confines of race, class and gender oppression' (Collins, 1990: 93). Black British Academics fulfils the same need to be culturally connected in order to feel whole; encapsulated in the *Ubuntu* philosophy 'I am because we are, and since we are therefore I am' (Nussbaum, 2003: 21). Black communities are important in providing platforms 'where safe discourse can potentially occur...' and 'a prime location for resisting objectification as the other' and developing 'a culture of resistance' (Collins, 1990: 95).

Conclusion

Self-definition and self-valuation are supported by values present in social relationships, such as community networks, family and that key element of Black women's culture, 'sisterhood': 'the interpersonal relationships that Black women share with each other' based on common experiences of oppression (Collins, 1986: S22), which promote 'solidarity and a sense of connection and community' (Oyewumi, 2003: 8). The support and encouragement of my sibling sisters have been vital components of my survival as an academic through the most challenging times. Throughout my journey, I have also maintained close sister relationships with fellow women of colour academics and these are immensely important. One relationship in particular is with a beloved friend, colleague and associate. We engage in weekly discussions when time permits, during which we share and analyse our experiences as sisters, daughters, aunts, mothers, wives and, importantly, as Black women academics. Sometimes the stories are funny and we laugh, sometimes they are painful and we empathize and resolve to stand firm and support each other to rise above our oppression – and always to challenge the structures, systems and people at the source of our oppression. I attribute my resilience, determination and motivation to survive and thrive to my family, community networks and, especially, to my sister friends. These relationships are acknowledged as vitally important in Black feminist theory, not only for the empathy expressed through dialogue, or through the acquisition of experiential knowledge, but also through the consciousness such interactions foster, which sharpen our understandings of oppression and influence our actions (Collins, 1986).

References

Ahmed, S. (2007) '"You end up doing the document rather than doing the doing": Diversity, race equality and the politics of documentation'. *Ethnic and Racial Studies*, 30 (4), 590–609.

— (2009) 'Embodying diversity: Problems and paradoxes for Black feminists'. *Race Ethnicity and Education*, 12 (1), 41–52.

Alexander-Floyd, N.G. (2012) 'Disappearing acts: Reclaiming intersectionality in the social sciences in a post-Black feminist era'. *Feminist Formations*, 24 (1), 1–25.

Alfred, M.V. (2001) 'Expanding theories of career development: Adding the voices of African American women in the white academy'. *Adult Education Quarterly*, 51 (2), 108–27.

Bhopal, K. and Jackson, J. (2013) *The Experiences of Black and Minority Ethnic Academics: Multiple identities and career progression.* Southampton: University of Southampton.

Bilge, S. (2013) 'Intersectionality undone: Saving intersectionality from feminist intersectionality studies'. *Du Bois Review: Social Science Research on Race*, 10 (2), 405–24.

Carastathis, A. (2014) 'The concept of intersectionality in feminist theory'. *Philosophy Compass*, 9 (5), 304–14.

Carby, H.V. (1996) 'White woman listen! Black feminism and the boundaries of sisterhood'. In Baker, H.A., Diawara, M. and Lindeborg, R.H. (eds) *Black British Cultural Studies: A reader*. Chicago: University of Chicago Press, 61–86.

Collins, P.H. (1986) 'Learning from the outsider within: The sociological significance of Black feminist thought'. *Social Problems*, 33 (6), S14–S32.

— (1989) 'The social construction of black feminist thought'. *Signs: Journal of Women in Culture and Society*, 14 (4), 745–73.

— (1990) *Black Feminist Thought: Knowledge, consciousness, and the politics of empowerment*. London: Routledge.

Craig, M.L. (2006) 'Race, beauty, and the tangled knot of a guilty pleasure'. *Feminist Theory*, 7 (2), 159–77.

Eze, E.C. (ed.) (1997) *Race and the Enlightenment: A reader*. Malden, MA: Blackwell.

Gabriel, D. (2013a) 'Self-empowerment is the best way to defeat racism in academia'. *The Independent*, 22 April. Online. www.independent.co.uk/student/news/self-empowerment-is-the-best-way-to-defeat-racism-in-academia-8582702.html (accessed 10 January 2017).

— (2013b) 'Ethnic and gender inequalities in postgraduate study still aren't being addressed'. *The Independent*, 2 May. Online. www.independent.co.uk/student/postgraduate/postgraduate-study/ethnic-and-gender-inequalities-in-postgraduate-study-still-arent-being-addressed-8599466.html (accessed 10 January 2017).

— (2013c) 'Race equality in academia: Time to establish Black studies in the UK?'. *The Guardian*, 25 July. Online. www.theguardian.com/higher-education-network/blog/2013/jul/25/race-equality-academia-curriculum?commentpage=1 (accessed 10 January 2017).

— (2013d) 'Race equality in academia: We've got a huge way to go'. *The Independent*, 5 August. Online. www.independent.co.uk/student/istudents/race-equality-in-academia-weve-got-a-huge-way-to-go-8746877.html (accessed 10 January 2017).

— (2014) *Blogging while Black and British: An exploratory study on the use of blogs as social, cultural and counterhegemonic practice*. PhD thesis, University of Salford.

— (2016a) 'In critique of blackface and institutional indifference to racism'. Online. http://blackbritishacademics.co.uk/2016/07/05/in-critique-of-blackface-and-institutional-indifference-to-racism (accessed 10 January 2017).

— (2016b) 'Another year in the life of an early career researcher'. Online. http://deborahgabriel.com/2016/12/03/another-year-in-the-life-of-an-early-career-researcher (accessed 10 January 2017).

Gervais, S.J., Bernard, P., Klein, O. and Allen, J. (2013) 'Toward a unified theory of objectification and dehumanization'. In Gervais, S.J. (ed.) *Objectification and (De)Humanization: 60th Nebraska Symposium on Motivation*. New York: Springer, 1–23.

Griffin, R.A. (2012) 'I AM an angry Black woman: Black feminist autoethnography, voice, and resistance'. *Women's Studies in Communication*, 35 (2), 138–57.

hooks, b. (1989) *Talking Back: Thinking feminist, thinking black*. Boston: South End Press.

Jones, C. (2006) 'Falling between the cracks: What diversity means for black women in higher education'. *Policy Futures in Education*, 4 (2), 145–59.

Jordan, W.D. (1962) 'American chiaroscuro: The status and definition of mulattoes in the British colonies'. *William and Mary Quarterly*, 19 (2), 183–200.

Karenga, M. (1980) *Kawaida Theory: An introductory outline*. Inglewood, CA: Kaiwaida Publications.

Leonardo, Z. (2004) 'The color of supremacy: Beyond the discourse of "white privilege"'. *Educational Philosophy and Theory*, 36 (2), 137–52.

Loughnan, S., Haslam, N., Murnane, T., Vaes, J., Reynolds, C. and Suitner, C. (2010) 'Objectification leads to depersonalization: The denial of mind and moral concern to objectified others'. *European Journal of Social Psychology*, 40 (5), 709–17.

Nussbaum, B. (2003) 'Ubuntu: Reflections of a South African on our common humanity'. *Reflections*, 4 (4), 21–6.

Oyewumi, O. (ed.) (2003) *African Women and Feminism: Reflecting on the politics of sisterhood*. Trenton, NJ: Africa World Press.

Puwar, N. (2004) 'Fish in or out of water: A theoretical framework for race and the space of academia'. In Law, I., Phillips, D. and Turney, L. (eds) *Institutional Racism in Higher Education*. Stoke-on-Trent: Trentham Books, 49–58.

Scheurich, J.J. (1993) 'Toward a white discourse on white racism'. *Educational Researcher*, 22 (8), 5–10.

Thomas, K.M., Mack, D.A., Williams, K.L. and Perkins, L.A. (1999) 'Career development strategies and experiences of "outsiders within" in academe'. *Journal of Career Development*, 26 (1), 51–67.

Wright, C., Thompson, S. and Channer, Y. (2007) 'Out of place: Black women academics in British universities'. *Women's History Review*, 16 (2), 145–62.

Ziegert, J.C. and Hanges, P.J. (2005) 'Employment discrimination: The role of implicit attitudes, motivation, and a climate for racial bias'. *Journal of Applied Psychology*, 90 (3), 553–62.

Chapter 3

'One in a million': A journey of a post-colonial woman of colour in the White academy

Heidi Safia Mirza

Introduction: On being endangered

To be 'one in a million', an exotic token, an institutional symbol, a mentor and confidante, and a 'natural expert' on all things to do with 'race', is something that many Black and ethnicized post-colonial women of colour* recount in their careers in the academy (Ahmed, 2009; Essed, 2000; hooks, 1994; Maylor, 2010; Mirza, 1995; Mohanty, 1993; Razack, 1998; Simmonds, 1997; Spivak, 1993; Wane, 2009; Williams, 1991). I proudly belong to a generation of British post-colonial women who have struggled together in the world of the academy in Britain since the 1970s. We have established a small but important community of women scholars of colour in UK universities with many of us now actually professors. Maybe I was deluded by our newfound status and assumed that a few Black and minority ethnic women having a place in the academy means we are no longer considered an endangered species! However, data from the Higher Education Statistics Authority (HESA) (Black British Academics, 2016) shows that only 110 of the UK's 19,630 professors are Black, and only 30 are Black women. In a brave new world of globalization and internationalization in higher education, academia in post-colonial and now so-called 'post-race' Britain still remains hideously White and still not a place you expect to find many Black bodies.

---

* In this chapter, I use 'Black women' to denote global women of African descent, but also recognize its history as a British collective political term that embraces post-colonial 'women of colour' who share similar racialized marginal locations in relation to the violent oppression of colonization and structural instigation of White privilege (Mirza, 1997, 2009). I also use the term 'Black and ethnicized women' as being *or becoming* 'ethnicized' brings into play the power relations that inform and structure the gaze of the 'other'. While official policy terms such as 'Black and minority ethnic women' denote the social construction of difference through visible racial (Black) and cultural (ethnic) markers, they do not emphasize the *process* of racial objectification (see Bhavnani *et al.*, 2005).

Being a Black female body 'out of place' in White institutions has emotional and psychological costs to the bearer of that difference. For Black and post-colonial women of colour, it is impossible to 'escape the body' and its constructions and reconstructions as we daily negotiate our embodied social situations in White institutions. The notion of 'embodied intersectionality' (Mirza, 2009, 2013) has helped me to make sense of my struggle and situate what defines the materiality of my 'affective' educational experience. Felly Nweko Simmonds (1997: 227) writes of this embodied Black female experience, saying, 'The world I inhabit as a [Black] academic is a white world ... in this white world I am a fresh water fish that swims in sea water. I feel the weight of the water on my body.' It is a powerful statement about the personal costs of marginality for Black women and the profound experiences we have when moving between 'worlds' of difference in higher education. As Black feminists we need to ask questions continually about what shapes these worlds and how we are implicated in the deeply racist and sexist discourses through the patterns of inclusion and exclusion that frame our 'choices' and participation (Mirza, 2015). As I shall reveal in my unfolding story, my personal experience of daily indifference, sexual harassment and racial marginalization is not just individuated happenchance in my own particular life, but symbolic of the systemic nature of gendered racialization as revealed by a Black woman's narrative through time and space in higher education.

Telling stories: Autoethnography for Black feminists

In this chapter, I draw on my personalized 'embodied' narrative to demonstrate the intersectional processes of 'being and becoming' a gendered and raced subject of academic and educational discourse. Documenting 'our experience' as women of colour through autoethnography reveals the ways in which the regulatory discursive power and privilege of Whiteness in our institutions are performed or exercised in the everyday material world of the socially constructed Black and post-colonial woman of colour. Autoethnography is a powerful tool as individual stories illuminate the collective effects of discursive processes, such as all-consuming Whiteness, that construct our social and political worlds (Pennington, 2007). Black feminism complements this methodology because, as a theory, it seeks to make sense of the Black woman's symbolic and narrative struggle over the defining materiality of her 'othered' bodily experience. Race, class, gender and sexuality collide in my narrative to reveal my 'embodied intersectionality'. Visible difference written on the body means Black women are drawn into sharing our own 'very private information' to make a point. Black women can't afford the luxury enjoyed by White male theorists who need not admit their unmarked bodies into theory (Ahmed, 2014; Burton, 2015). They have the privilege to opt for 'silence' about their own private information. Black women, on the other hand, and those marginal 'others' who are marked by their disability and sexuality, *live in and with* the body. They are compelled to share a certain degree of private information just so they can be seen and heard and so gain a modicum of 'legitimacy' in the White heteronormative, patriarchal world. But in so doing the newly 'visible' woman of colour becomes exposed, vulnerable and open to individual scrutiny and judgement.

In writing this autoethnography, as I put my words on the page here, I find they are revealing, embarrassing, discontinuous and cleansing all at once. I am compelled to ask 'Who am I? What do I want the world to know about me? Who is my audience and how honest can I be? What is the truth about "my life"? Would I have said something different about my academic life three years ago when I was on a high starting a new job, or a month ago when I resigned after things turned raw and sour?' These questions demonstrate the destabilizing effects of autobiographical narrative and its methodological boundaries, which empower the teller's interpretation of the past (Cosslett *et al.*, 2000). My personal mantra that I tell my students has always been 'we *must* tell our stories, or others will tell them for us … our stories must be told!'

My academic life has spanned more than three decades. My first book, *Young Female and Black* (1992), was a small-scale ethnography of young Caribbean women in a London school. As a young woman, I made the same journey as the young women I documented in the research had in their own lives. I grew up in Trinidad in the 1960s and migrated to England in the 1970s where I went to school in London. So in a direct way it was a study about my own life and experiences – it was, in a sense, an autoethnography by the back door! I wanted to research and write about second-generation Caribbean young women like myself in British schools, and the interplay between career choices, aspirations and educational structures in an overtly racist time. The book, which was my PhD, was in effect both an academic and an autobiographical journey. On reflection, exploring the exclusionary practices of the gendered racism that I saw around me was a cathartic process. In this sense, academic writing based on autobiography can be like a mask. You can use academic theory and academic conventions to articulate, in a very objective and distanced way, something you have experienced yourself, without really naming it or implicating yourself emotionally in it. Such a reflexive and experiential positioning of 'the self' in theory is fundamental to a Black feminist position and my ensuing narrative is grounded in this theoretical standpoint.

Crossing over: A journey into the 'heart of whiteness'

Kathleen Casey (1993), in her classic and moving book on the struggles and sacrifices of urban school teachers in the United States, brilliantly sums up so much of my own journey in and through academia. Of the African-American student teachers, she writes:

> Young black women set off into the white world carrying expectations of mythic proportions ... their odysseys, they believe will transform their lives ... but separated from their cultural communities these young women's passages turn out to be isolated individual journeys ... into the heart of whiteness.
>
> (Casey, 1993: 132)

For me, this simple eloquent passage illustrates the complex multidimensional embodied world that Black and ethnicized women simultaneously inhabit as educators, researchers and mentors when we operate at both the *heart* and the *margins* of our overwhelmingly White academic institutions. Being an outsider-within in the elite and privileged spaces of academia is a hard space to inhabit. Sometimes I am shocked by the deeply racist comments I hear in everyday life in the higher echelons of our so-called 'civilized' 'diverse' universities. When I was on a search committee for the appointment of a professorial chair in a prestigious university I was sent an email by a senior White male academic about the applications. He stated that there had been several applicants, who were described in terms of their research (they were not racialized), and then one application was from a 'not very incredible Indian'. Why was 'the Indian' racialized and none of the others? What difference did it make that he was Indian? What was I being 'told' in this coded message? Was it that 'all Indians (like refugees) want to come to England and will try anything'? Or that other familiar racist trope: 'Indian qualifications are not very good, and anyway an Indian can never be as good as a White (British) academic'. Why did the White male academic who sent the email not think about what he was saying to me – a woman of Indo-Caribbean heritage? Was it because, even though I am one of them (an Indian), I am now 'one of us' (an 'honorary White' who can speak their language)? Why did he say it at all? Maybe because he could?

Patricia Williams, the inspirational African-American law professor, speaks of the trauma such everyday incursions into your selfhood engender. I find inspiration in her womanist words of wisdom, which enable me to articulate the unspeakable paralysing anguish and pain that racism and sexism can engender. She writes:

> There are moments in my life when I feel as though part of me is missing. There are days when I feel so invisible that I can't remember the day of the week it is, when I feel so manipulated that I can't remember my own name, when I feel so lost and angry that I can't speak a civil word to the people who love me best. These are times I catch sight of my reflection in store windows and I am surprised to see the whole person looking back … I have to close my eyes at such times and remember myself, draw an internal pattern that is smooth and whole.
>
> (Williams, 1991, quoted in hooks, 1994: 74)

bell hooks (1991) counsels us that, as Black feminists, we need to courageously expose our 'wounds' of struggle and theorize from a place of pain. While theorizing from a 'place of pain' gives us healing words to recover ourselves from the anguish that racist and sexist oppression create in daily life, such 'claims' to affective experiences can be appropriated by the privileged White majority (Applebaum, 2008). For example, when I was appointed Professor of Racial Equality Studies, the first Chair of its kind in Britain, a White male professor leaned in to me at the celebration drinks and whispered bitterly in my ear, "Well, they are giving Chairs to anyone for anything these days." His 'White hurt' invoked by my 'unfair' success is a pernicious 'post-race' discourse that accompanies the multicultural backlash we are witnessing now. 'White hurt' sees 'equality' for people of colour as an unfair social advantage rooted in policies of political correctness. The underlying belief now is that those who are 'really discriminated' against are the displaced White majority.

In our meritocratic societies, where the illusion of 'raw', 'natural' achievement is valued above social justice, there is always a question mark hanging over our appointments and academic ability. It allows self-doubt to creep in late at night, 'Is that what they are really thinking? Am I a case of "special pleading", no more than a "politically correct appointment" made under the cosh of the dreaded draconian institutional "equality and diversity" policies?' Nagging self-doubt is not an easy burden to bear in the competitive space of higher education, with its slick language of corporate multiculturalism and individuating rights-based approaches to equality and diversity.

In this hostile 'post-race' climate, Black British feminists have to navigate the tricky terrain of a 'diversity industry' which reifies difference as something that exists 'in' the bodies of the raced and ethnicized others. The very arrival of the 'Black/othered' body into White/normative organizations is used as evidence that spaces of Whiteness and privilege no longer exist, where just using the word 'diversity' is seen to 'do' positive things for the institution. Visual images of 'colourful' happy faces are used to show how the university has embraced difference. My 'happy' face appeared on the front of the university's website – even though every week I asked for it to be taken down, it still kept popping up! My hard-won achievements, books, lectures and awards were claimed and appropriated as a sign of the university's diversity and, hence, success. Ahmed (2012) eloquently argues that, in this climate of 'happy diversity', to speak about racism is to introduce unwanted 'bad feelings', and she counsels Black feminists to remain 'sore' and 'angry' and refuse to be appropriated through institutional policy and practice as the 'happy objects' of diversity in our universities.

Workshops in equality and diversity are never 'safe spaces' for people of colour who are invited to 'tell their story'. In the latest incarnation of bureaucratic anti-racist training, concerns about institutional racism in the 1990s have given way to lessons in 'unconscious bias' (ECU, 2013). However, in an inherently violent colonial racial order, race dialogue in White privileged frameworks means that, in reality, 'blacks disappear to give way to educating whites' (Leonardo and Porter, 2010). In a workshop I once attended, a Muslim graduate student recounted how her husband, a qualified medical doctor, was experiencing racial discrimination when trying to get a job. A senior White male member of the group, an established academic, 'supportively' piped up and said 'don't worry love ... it wouldn't happen to you as you are so attractive'. All the Black and ethnicized women in the group gasped. In that one moment, they were reduced to no more than their embodied 'otherness' – mute visible objects, empty scripts for him to write his story. His racist and sexist comment was made possible by the unspoken power of his Whiteness and privileged masculinity and the inherent entitlement such intersectional positioning bestows on his authoritative gaze. This is why we must tell *our own* stories – or they will be told *for* us ... and *about* us!

There are many ways in which Black ethnicized female bodies are seen when they do not represent the 'racial somatic norm' within White institutions. As Puwar (2001) first explained, there is 'disorientation', a double-take as you enter a room, as if you are not supposed to be there. You are noticed and it is uncomfortable. Like walking into a pub in a town where you don't live. There is confusion, as you are not the natural expected occupant of that role. I know this well; in many meetings, even though I am a professor, I have been mistaken for the coffee lady. For fun, I often pour the coffee (in a cup … not on the floor!), and then watch their faces as I sit down at the table in the board room! Even now, students do a double-take when they realize I am the 'expert' professor taking the class. Second, there is 'infantalization', where you are not only pigeon-holed as the resident 'race expert' (I am often asked to perform the duties of the 'diversity officer'), but you are also seen as less capable of being in authority. This can mean you are assumed to be more junior than you are. Indeed, I have been told to get off the departmental photocopier as it is for academics, not administrators.

Third, there is the 'burden of invisibility' or 'hyper-surveillance'. Here you are viewed suspiciously and, unlike favoured White colleagues, any mistakes are picked up and seen as a sign of gross incompetence or misplaced authority. You have to work harder for recognition outside the confines of stereotypical expectations, and you can suffer disciplinary measures and disappointment if you do not meet expectations in your work performance … and in my case, even if you do, you may still be deemed 'redundant'! In higher education, surveillance strategies have become increasingly important ways to 'police' Black and ethnicized women as they enter institutional spaces of Whiteness in the increasingly devalued public sphere from which they were hitherto barred in times of overt institutionalized racism (Collins, 1998: 39). To be seen to be 'acculturated' is important for Black and ethnicized women, as 'standing out' can invoke deep feelings of need, rejection and anxiety within the 'White other' (Ahmed, 2005).

Our survival strategy is often to work hard at 'being seen' to be assimilated, though we pay a high price for it. We think about what to wear, how we 'come across', the way we speak (as the University Orator I have learnt to 'speak like them'). At an important funding meeting, I was asked by a senior White male academic if I was *'really* one of the few female professors of colour in Britain?' He was incredulous and curious. I sat in polite silence while in response he excitedly regaled me, non-stop for half an hour, about all the Black women academics he knew … and how well he knew them, with details (often mixing up names!) of intimacies and gossip. I felt embarrassed, negated and erased by his profoundly unreflexive sense of entitlement to speak over me and through me. By asserting his 'knowledge' about me and my 'kind', he sought to 'know me better than I know myself'. We ran out of time in the meeting which he dominated – I never got to voice my ideas and contribute to the important agenda. Dignity is a high price to pay for survival in the academy. As Patricia Williams (1991) says, you do so easily lose a piece of yourself in our journey into the 'heart of whiteness'.

From shame to action: Naming racialized sexual harassment in the academy

There is another irony to heightened visibility for the 'invisible' women of colour in our polite and gentle corridors of the elite academy. National surveys of ethnic minorities in higher education have found Black and minority ethnic women are more likely than any other group to report being the victim of sexual harassment and discrimination at work (Bhopal and Jackson, 2013; ECU, 2011). This raises many questions about the safety of women of colour in public spaces. In my 30 years in higher education, as a student but also as faculty, I have witnessed and been subjected to endemic and sustained sexual harassment. There's not an institution or time when I have not seen it. It oozes out of every lecture hall, lab, classroom, tutorial, eatery and office. Louise Morley's (2010) study of gender mainstreaming in universities in Tanzania and Ghana shows how rumours of sexual exchange undermine and diminish Black women's achievements. She documents how, when women gain access to male spaces, the soothing belief among the men is, 'of course it is only because of their "prostitution" that women get in and do well!' In a self-fulfilling prophecy, they reconfirm to themselves that women are still not yet ready to occupy an equal place in higher education.

Sexist patriarchal practices are universal in higher education and have different forms in different times and places, but I think the more times change the more they stay the same. In the 1970s, White male lecturers in Britain (and they were all White and male!) had cushions on the floor and would invite you to 'lay lady lay' (à la Bob Dylan) … with an accompanying spliff and the promises of the benefits of being in the in-crowd! As a young woman of colour, the normalcy of your non-personhood meant that you were no more than a tasty piece of exotic brown meat – to be sampled and discarded. It was in the 1980s that I first noticed more casual grooming. Collectivities of men – lecturers, professors even – flocking around the photocopier laughing as they discussed the latest intake of female undergraduates, the next piece of ripe 'juicy ass', and who and how they would seduce them. This was a lad's game in which young women's bodies were being bought and sold for marks and favours. The sense of male entitlement and objectification of women as 'sport' was complete. I had letters sent to me about squeezing my tits with offers of condoms. I was stalked at conferences, followed home, attacked in cars, locked in rooms, and thrown up against walls in elevators – all for the sake of a disgusting, pathetic grope. When I rejected these advances, I was told I was nothing, nobody, and would be ousted as the academic fraud I am – and that as a woman of colour I was lucky to be there – a privileged position I was warned I did not want to jeopardize.

Individual experiences of sexual harassment are rarely allowed to do their work to change the status quo, except through the courage of the few who stand up and make a difference – those pioneers who sacrifice their careers and reputations and lives challenging the institutional systems. There are many historical precedents where women of colour courageously stood up to sexual harassment. It is a messy, tangled, gendered, classed and raced business. African-American feminists Kimberlé Crenshaw (1993) and Patricia Hill Collins (1998) write about the case of Professor Anita Hill, who in 1991 broke the taboo of silence about sexual harassment in the African-American community by calling out Clarence Thomas, the Black Republican Supreme Court judge candidate who openly sexually harassed her and others. In the horrors and injustices that unfolded in the hearings, Anita Hill's 'race' was trumped by her sex. She suffered what Crenshaw calls intersectional disempowerment. She fell between the polarization of Black men on the one hand and White women on the other, invisible in the separate rhetorical spaces of political anti-racism and feminism. There were no narrative tropes, no stories of Black women as victims of simultaneous racial and sexual discrimination that enabled her to gain a fair hearing. She was seen as a Black middle-class 'lady overachiever', out of place in a world of Black working-class 'welfare queens', who was willing to trade her 'honour' for her career. She was also characterized as a 'traitor-to-the-race', vilified for using her sexuality to undermine the Black community by entrapping a Black brother. Thomas conjured up the racist guilt of the White establishment in his defence, provocatively accusing them of a 'high-tech lynching'. Constructing himself as the victim of a racist attack, he successfully deflected his actions as a sexual predator. Anita Hill paid a high price for her courage, which left her the loser in the ultimate game of patriarchal power and male solidarity. Clarence Thomas, backed by his White Republican brothers, won the case and secured his position. Is this what happens to you when you take a stand?

By the 1990s, I came up against more organized grooming. These were men in 'packs' with ring leaders operating in departments with trained 'gofers' who were sent out hunting to bring back female prey, many of whom were South East Asian, Black, mixed-race and working-class female students, who were seen as no more than racialized 'exotic' jezebels (hooks, 1991) and thus particularly sexually available. In the 2000s, these packs morphed into more sophisticated 'harems' that complemented the desperate needs of failing professors unable to sustain their careers given the unyielding demands of neoliberal performance in higher education. Smart female students or early career researchers were seduced into giving up their intellectual labour in return for 'love', to serve male (and sometimes female) academics in fear of failing and exposing their unproductive careers. In the war of post-feminist attrition, I have seen how these women are isolated, picked off as mentally ill, needy, serial complainers, and mischief makers, punished with no or failed degrees, careers in ruins and palmed off with therapy. The fate of the perpetrators? No more than a slap on the wrist, unpaid leave, early retirement often with a handsome payoff. Burying the human evidence appears to be the higher education sector's institutional strategy. The reputational profile or 'honour' of the university is the ultimate currency in market-driven higher education. But what a price *we* women pay!

I like to think of myself as a survivor, but unlike my brave sisters who have outed their perpetrators I find my experiences so painful that they live deep in my soul in a place of shame. Writing about it now, I can begin to exhale – it is by unlocking the door of shame that we can begin to understand the affect or emotions that sustain and feed raced/gendered sexual harassment endemic in our institutions. To do this, we need to ask difficult questions like, 'how does shame become such a powerful silencer, a compatriot, a "bedfellow" of institutional acts of racist gender domination and oppression?' 'Why do we engage in regimes of self-regulation that collaborate with systems of racialized sexual power?' Sexual harassment and violence cut across all cultures and predicate themselves on the insidious dyad of 'honour and shame'. My research on honour-based violence in South Asian communities shows how honour and its mirror image, shame, are fundamental to the survival of oppressive patriarchal regimes (Meetoo and Mirza, 2007). We like to think that honour-based ideologies belong 'out there' to other cultures: 'hot-blooded', vengeful Mediterranean or Latin types, or in these Islamophobic times, 'barbaric' Muslims who must cover or avenge their women's 'honour'. We say, comforting ourselves, 'Surely honour is not part of our Western liberal democratic societies where women have freedom, agency and choice?'

By invoking shame to get to the root of the reproduction of sexual harassment, I am not sanctioning or celebrating victimhood, but rather asking us to rethink the power of the self and affect, in understanding the emotional cement that keeps the 'walls' (Ahmed, 2012) of everyday racialized gender power relations sedimented and in place. The shame of being vulnerable, the shame of being a victim, of being different, the shame of your sex, the shame of rejection, of not being loved, of not belonging – Ahmed (2005) explains that the 'bad feelings' shame brings are attributed to oneself rather than the object or other who is the cause of the 'bad feeling'. So when you feel you have failed (to achieve your ideal, where honour elusively resides), you experience shame as hurt and anger which you turn inward to the self. Elspeth Probyn (2005) says shame makes you sick. Writing about shame right now is painful, it involves exposure of the intimacies of the self in public. It gets into your body, and it can make you sick. Cancer has made me sick but – as Maya Angelou (1984) says in *I Know Why the Caged Bird Sings* – 'and still I rise!'

Conclusion: Race, gender and 'embodied intersectionality' in telling tales

Through an autoethnography of my 'embodied intersectionality', I have explored the ways in which my raced and gendered human agency frames my struggle for life chances, opportunities and well-being in academia. 'Embodied intersectionality' as a concept gives me the theoretical tools to help me make sense of my journey. It provides an intersectional framework in which race, class, gender and other social divisions come together simultaneously and are theorized as lived realities on and through the body (Mirza, 2009, 2013). By asking, 'How do class, race and gender distinctions structure my subjectivity as an "othered" woman of colour in our overwhelmingly dominant White places of teaching and learning?', my journey reveals the multiple ways in which structures of power embodied by the White male other operate 'affectively' to reproduce racialized gendered divisions and frame our academic opportunities. By asking, 'How does my "embodied" story illuminate what it means to be a professional Black female body out of place in a White institution?', my personal narrative opens up to public scrutiny the corporeal reality of deeply hidden feelings of frustration, pain, anger, shame and sadness. To be misrecognized (as a race expert), or hyper-visible (as 'one in a million'); to be 'known better than you know yourself' (to be rendered voiceless); to be ignored or have your ability questioned (are you really a professor?); to 'be seen to be happy' and fit in (don't offend or you will be excluded!); and to survive sexual predators only to be silenced through shame (as an exotic other). Naming our experiences whatever they are, no matter how hard they are to write about, is vital if Black and ethnicized women are to be recognized by White colleagues in White institutions, firstly as individuals, and secondly as educated, knowledgeable and competent academics.

While autoethnography is a vital strategy of Black and post-colonial feminist theorizing, we have to be ever-vigilant of invoking it as a means to interrogate the embodied nature of systemic institutionalized discriminatory practices. While our stories can illuminate, from a personal standpoint, the processes of 'being and becoming' a gendered and raced subject of academic and educational discourse, placing the 'self' in the text can also be our undoing. By unveiling our inner-most life stories, Black and ethnicized women risk becoming objects of the public gaze. Our strategies for resistance become 'known', and 'objective' knowledge about us is formed. However, revealing the social world through our 'other ways of knowing' does not mean we valorize mere experience and claim our stories to be a *social fact* (Applebaum, 2008). Rather we use experience as 'standpoint', offering a mediated interpretation of the social world. The seductive affective workings of White patriarchal privilege and power can be revealed through our critical analysis of our stories. Drawing on a 'Black feminist standpoint', as hooks (1991) explains, produces radical 'other ways of knowing' that can displace and subvert our traditional position of marginality and exclusion as Black and post-colonial women of colour in the academy. She writes:

> Marginality is a central location for the production of a counter hegemonic discourse – it is found in the words, habits and the way one lives ... It is a site one clings to even when moving to the centre ... it nourishes our capacity to resist ... It is an inclusive space where we recover ourselves, where we move in solidarity to erase the category coloniser/colonised.
>
> (hooks, 1991: 149–150)

I do find an empowering message in hooks' feminist words of wisdom. She gives me a way in to understanding the shifts in my relative positions of power and privilege, as I have moved from the 'margin in to the centre' on my journey to 'become' one of the first and few female professors of colour in Britain. To survive and succeed in this journey, I have evolved a 'quiet' subversive radical pedagogic practice that allows me to operate within, between, under and alongside the dominant educational discourse. Through feminist 'acts of care' and 'other ways of knowing', I, like my Black and ethnicized sisters in higher education, work to keep alive our communities' collective belief and desire in the power of education to transform our lives. Such a Black feminist pedagogy of hope and educational transformation enacted from within the 'walls' of our historically racist institutions may appear 'conservative' on the surface, with its focus on inclusion and dialogue with the mainstream (Mirza, 2009; Ali, 2010). However, for Black and post-colonial women of colour, education is not simply a mechanism through which individuals are unconsciously subjected to the dominant ideological system but rather, as Paulo Freire (2004) argues, it is the terrain on which we acquire consciousness of our position and struggle. From where I sit, Black and ethnicized women educators in academia have developed a positive sense of their space on the margin and through a process of self-actualization we strategically rationalize our situation and opportunities, and survive.

The academy is a difficult place for Black and post-colonial feminists, but it can also be a site of privilege, influence and joy, especially when bright-eyed Black and minority ethnic students enter our classrooms on their 'odysseys of self-discovery'. While Black female academics in Britain are still 'one in a million', ironically, in times of economic austerity and high tuition fees, working-class Black and minority ethnic students still express their 'educational desire' (Mirza, 2009) by coming to university in large numbers. They eagerly fill my classes to capacity, choosing to do non-vocational courses like my MA on Race, Gender and Social Justice, even in these neoliberal instrumentalist times. Racism is alive and kicking, and these students are aware of it. It is their lived experience, and they are angry about their enduring marginality and disadvantages despite the overwhelming, self-satisfied, bureaucratic rhetoric of institutional 'equality and diversity' we endure in so-called 'post-race times'. Through social media and campus protests, we are witnessing a generation of hopeful, confident young Black and ethnicized women and men rising up as the 'new Black and post-colonial intellectuals' of our times. There is a real sense of 'conscientization' among them (Freire, in McLaren and Leonard, 1993)! From the bottom up, in student-led new social movements, they are strategically engaging against racism in higher education by challenging the unspoken dominance of White knowledge in the university curriculum with calls to 'decolonize pedagogy' and teaching practice. Their organic global social movements, such as *#whyismycurriculumwhite*, *#whyisn'tmyprofessorblack*, *#Rhodesmustfall*, and *#IamtooOxford*, demonstrate the burgeoning of an empowering and collective Black and ethnicized student 'post-race' voice, mobilized in the fight against racism and gender discrimination, which is as strong as ever in the higher education system. I am with them all the way!

References

Ahmed, S. (2005) *The Cultural Politics of Emotion*. Edinburgh: Edinburgh University Press.

— (2009) 'Embodying diversity: Problems and paradoxes for black feminists'. *Race Ethnicity and Education*, 12 (1), 41–52.

— (2012) *On Being Included: Racism and diversity in institutional life*. Durham, NC: Duke University Press.

— (2014) 'White men'. *Feminist Killjoys*, 4 November. Online. http://feministkilljoys.com/2014/11/04/white-men (accessed 20 January 2017).

Ali, S. (2010) 'Black feminist praxis: Some reflections on pedagogies and politics in higher education'. In Mirza, H.S. and Joseph, C. (eds) *Black and Postcolonial Feminisms in New Times: Researching educational inequalities*. London: Routledge, 79–86.

Angelou, M. (1984) *I Know Why the Caged Bird Sings*. London: Virago Press.

Applebaum, B. (2008) '"Doesn't my experience count?": White students, the authority of experience and social justice pedagogy'. *Race Ethnicity and Education*, 11 (4), 405–14.

Bhavnani, R., Mirza, H.S. and Meetoo, V. (2005) *Tackling the Roots of Racism: Lessons for success*. Bristol: Policy Press.

Bhopal, K. and Jackson, J. (2013) *The Experiences of Black and Minority Ethnic Academics: Multiple identities and career progression*. Southampton: University of Southampton.

Black British Academics (2016) 'HESA statistics professors by race and gender'. Online. http://blackbritishacademics.co.uk/focus/hesa-statistics-professors-by-race-and-gender (accessed 29 July 2017).

Burton, S. (2015) 'The monstrous "White theory boy": Symbolic capital, pedagogy and the politics of knowledge'. *Sociological Research Online*, 20 (3), Article 14. Online. www.socresonline.org.uk/20/3/14.html (accessed 20 March 2017).

Casey, K. (1993) *I Answer with My Life: Life histories of women teachers working for social change*. New York: Routledge.

Collins, P.H. (1998) *Fighting Words: Black women and the search for justice*. Minneapolis: University of Minnesota Press.

Cosslett, T., Lury, C. and Summerfield, P. (eds) (2000) *Feminism and Autobiography: Texts, theories, methods*. London: Routledge.

Crenshaw, K. (1993) 'Whose story is it, anyway? Feminist and antiracist appropriations of Anita Hill'. In Morrison, T. (ed.) *Race-ing Justice, En-gendering Power: Essays on Anita Hill, Clarence Thomas, and the construction of social reality*. London: Chatto and Windus, 402–36.

ECU (Equality Challenge Unit) (2011) *The Experience of Black and Minority Ethnic Staff in Higher Education in England*. London: Equality Challenge Unit.

— (2013) *Unconscious Bias and Higher Education*. London: Equality Challenge Unit.

Essed, P. (2000) 'Dilemmas in leadership: Women of colour in the academy'. *Ethnic and Racial Studies*, 23 (5), 888–904.

Freire, P. (2004) *Pedagogy of Indignation*. Boulder, CO: Paradigm.

hooks, b. (1991) *Yearning: Race, gender and cultural politics*. London: Turnaround.

— (1994) *Teaching to Transgress: Education as the practice of freedom*. New York: Routledge.

Leonardo, Z. and Porter, R.K. (2010) 'Pedagogy of fear: Toward a Fanonian theory of "safety" in race dialogue'. *Race Ethnicity and Education*, 13 (2), 139–57.

Maylor, U. (2010) 'Is it because I'm Black? A Black female research experience'. In Mirza, H.S. and Joseph, C. (eds) *Black and Postcolonial Feminisms in New Times: Researching educational inequalities*. London: Routledge, 53–64.

McLaren, P. and Leonard, P. (eds) (1993) *Paulo Freire: A critical encounter*. London: Routledge.

Meetoo, V. and Mirza, H.S. (2007) '"There is nothing 'honourable' about honour killings": Gender, violence and the limits of multiculturalism'. *Women's Studies International Forum*, 30 (3), 187–200.

Mirza, H.S. (1992) *Young, Female and Black*. London: Routledge.

— (1995) 'Black women in higher education: Defining a space/finding a place'. In Morley, L. and Walsh, V. (eds) *Feminist Academics: Creative agents for change*. London: Taylor and Francis, 145–55.

— (1997) *Black British Feminism: A reader*. London: Routledge.

— (2009) *Race, Gender and Educational Desire: Why Black women succeed and fail*. London: Routledge.

— (2013) '"A Second Skin": Embodied intersectionality, transnationalism and narratives of identity and belonging among Muslim women in Britain'. *Women's Studies International Forum*, 36, 5–15.

— (2015) '"Harvesting our collective intelligence": Black British feminism in post-race times'. *Women's Studies International Forum*, 51, 1–9.

Mohanty, C.T. (1993) 'On race and voice: Challenges for liberal education in the 1990s'. In Thompson, B.W. and Tyagi, S. (eds) *Beyond a Dream Deferred: Multicultural education and the politics of excellence*. Minneapolis: University of Minnesota Press, 41–65.

Morley, L. (2010) 'Gender mainstreaming: Myths and measurement in higher education in Ghana and Tanzania'. *Compare: A Journal of Comparative and International Education*, 40 (4), 533–50.

Pennington, J.L. (2007) 'Silence in the classroom/whispers in the halls: Autoethnography as pedagogy in white pre-service teacher education'. *Race Ethnicity and Education*, 10 (1), 93–113.

Probyn, E. (2005) *Blush: Faces of shame*. Minneapolis: University of Minnesota Press.

Puwar, N. (2001) 'The racialised somatic norm and the senior civil service'. *Sociology*, 35 (3), 651–70.

Razack, S.H. (1998) *Looking White People in the Eye: Gender, race, and culture in courtrooms and classrooms*. Toronto: University of Toronto Press.

Simmonds, F.N. (1997) 'My body, myself: How does a Black woman do sociology?'. In Mirza, H.S. (ed.) *Black British Feminism: A reader*. London: Routledge, 226–39.

Spivak, G.C. (1993) *Outside in the Teaching Machine*. New York: Routledge.

Wane, N.N. (2009) 'Black Canadian feminist thought: Perspectives on equity and diversity in the academy'. *Race Ethnicity and Education*, 12 (1), 65–77.

Williams, P.J. (1991) *The Alchemy of Race and Rights: Diary of a law professor*. Cambridge, MA: Harvard University Press.

Chapter 4

How do you feel? 'Well-being' as a deracinated strategic goal in UK universities

Shirley Anne Tate

Introduction

Employee 'well-being' is on the strategic agenda of every university in the UK as part of their people management framework. Well-being relates to those feelings that can be spoken, their generation through managerial relationalities and their governance within higher education institutions (HEIs). Each year, HEIs draw up strategies to assess departmental performance on this index, among others such as student recruitment, research income and student experience.

However, 'those feelings that can be spoken' already implies questions of power, governmentality and affective management, because some feelings are necessarily ruled out as unvoiceable. If there is already an unvoiceability regime in place, then only some answers will be recognized as acceptable when asked the question 'how do you feel?' about this or that aspect of your life as a Black woman university employee. Questions about and answers that voice the daily racism and racist micro-aggressions experienced by Black women academics will not be asked or recognized. What is interesting about well-being as a management strategy is its deracination, its lack of attention to the fact of racism and its negative impacts on the psyches and bodies of Black women academics, as lack of well-being is somatized. What would well-being strategies do if, in answer to the question of 'feeling', Black women answered, 'angry', 'upset', 'marginalized', 'racially discriminated against', 'ashamed', 'deep distrust', 'disgust', 'contempt'? What could these strategies possibly do with such negative affects (Ngai, 2005; Gutiérrez Rodríguez, 2010; Tate, 2014) produced from experiencing racism? Indeed, we could say that the objective of 'well-being' as a strategic aim is precisely not to do anything with these affects because that would be to admit that we inhabit racially toxic institutions that are inimical for everyone's psychic health. I do mean *everyone* here because, as Frantz Fanon (1986) and Lewis

Ricardo Gordon (1997) have shown, both those who suffer because of racism and those who are its perpetrators are irrevocably changed by the experience.

This chapter focuses on the negative affect of shame because of its very unvoiceability yet central place in Black women's experience of racism within academia. I look first at feelings of shame, before turning to the unvoiceability of negative feelings through institutional silencing and finally the impact of deracination on Black women academics' 'well-being' from the standpoint of having liveable lives at work. Let us begin with a colleague's narrated experience addressed to the general 'you' so as to implicate us all as we read and vicariously experience this racist shaming event.

Shame: Answering the question 'how do you feel?'

Your new head of department is a White feminist and sees feminism as your point of commonality. She asks you to a meeting when she takes up her position to tell you that you must reconcile with another White feminist who egregiously racially harassed you three years previously. You must reconcile because you have to work closely with her due to her departmental role but most importantly because she is 'the friend and colleague' of the head of department. You are told that whatever arrangements had been put into place to separate you in terms of office space from your racist harasser no longer hold and that she can be put anywhere in the building, so you should get used to that as the new approach because, after all, the person you see as your racist harasser 'just sent you some long emails'.

Let us pause for a moment and think about how we feel in terms of this racist shaming event and imagine what our colleague must have felt. Let us use those feelings to begin an analysis of how institutional racism works through micro-aggressions such as these because, as we know, daily interactions are the fabric of institutions (Boden, 1994). The idea that the racist harasser 'just sent you some long emails' denies the racism that was experienced all that time ago, the pain of which has been re-stimulated through its very denial in this narrated interaction from the past.

'Getting used to that as the new approach' immediately reinforces the certainty that the White feminist racist harasser has institutional support, and this again erases the fact that the racist incident occurred and was treated as such by a previous head of department who sought a spatial solution to prevent victimization and other further racist harms. The incident was dealt with then as an experience of racism. However, for the head of department to now say 'you must reconcile', when you have experienced egregious racism, denies the fact that racism happened. It diminishes the psychic harm experienced and the hurt feelings. This exposes you to more shame as your version of events is simply not being believed. Your harasser being set up as the head of department's 'friend and colleague' makes you both friendless and colleague-less in this encounter, and therefore removes you as a Black feminist academic from the location of both 'feminist' and 'academic'.

This whole interaction was a shaming one, enacted to shame this Black woman into a position where she doubts the veracity of her own recollections of harm, where she is made to feel like an outsider to the department, where she is reminded once again that White power is absolute and acts without qualms to favour those racialized as White, whatever their gender. I place myself in that room in that encounter meant to diminish Black women's personhood through its gaze of dissection (Yancy, 2008) and think that living with and through shame is part of the quotidian experience of Black women academics. None of us is exempt, irrespective of institutional status, and this is an important political message and a lesson that we must remember. We must remember it because even if we feel that we are included within White sociality and White networks, exceptionality procedures mean that our inclusion is partial. This is so because Whiteness and anti-Black woman racism dictate our very outsiderness, our position on the margins of organizational social life (Puwar, 2004; Rollock, 2012; Mirza, 1997).

However, as we know, we are not born shameful but we can be made to feel ashamed within toxic environments such as UK universities in which we are precariously located personally, professionally and politically because of anti-Black woman racism. The apparent White supremacist necessity to shame racialized others entails that shame is part of our working lives. We do not ask for it. After all, who would ask to suffer? The potential for shaming encounters such as the one above to occur at any time means that racist shame circulates uninhibited within institutions. It can no longer be related openly to what one looks like, to speaking aloud the fact of one's Blackness being problematic, since that would be openly racist and show a lack of civility in tolerant university settings. To say that our Blackness, our African descent, is a problem is to show the naked face of racism – which cannot be revealed if we are to keep the 'post-race' consensus in place (Goldberg, 2015).

Instead, UK HEIs operate within a colour-blind racism, a 'racism without racists' (Bonilla-Silva, 2014), which keeps the 'post-race' consensus in place without the words 'Look, a Black woman!' ever being spoken. This racism without racists can be shown in the shameful employment statistics within UK HEIs at present. Under-representation of Black and minority ethnic staff persists, even while there has been a year-on-year increase in Black and minority ethnic students (ECU, 2015). The numbers of Black and minority ethnic staff have increased from 4.8 per cent in 2003/04 to 6.7 per cent in 2013/14. In 2015, 8.3 per cent of the UK academic staff population were Black and minority ethnic, compared with 2.9 per cent of UK academic managers, directors and senior staff. Further, Black staff are still poorly paid and low status in comparison with White colleagues (ECU, 2015).

If phenotype cannot be openly used and we are within what Paul Gilroy (2004) calls a 'racial nomos' of discursive imperial ordering, how can racist shaming occur? Racist shaming cannot operate in the way Eve Sedgwick (2003) describes as being relevant for a hyper-reflexivity of the surface of the body because the shame sticks to that despised skin or feature. Racism cannot openly voice anti-Black woman phobia in terms of biology, because of the necessity to keep White neoliberal racism 'non-racist'. The impossible position of non-racism is necessary to continue the illusion that the racism we feel as Black women is of our own making and, in fact, that we are deluded because of our need to claim something that simply is not there and is only really in our imaginations. Go back here to the extract's 'just sent you some long emails' to get a handle on this last assertion that something is not there. 'Just' denies the racist content and micro-aggression of 'long emails', which are a favourite management tool to keep those of us who lack the necessary civility (Bhabha, 1994) in our institutional place of 'unlocation' (Mirza, 1997), where we remain perpetually 'bodies out of place' (Puwar, 2004). As we are 'unlocated/unlocatable' and 'out of place', racist shaming is a daily possibility for Black women academics. The implication of this is that since actions make institutions (Boden, 1994), White institutions are built on and sustained through racist shaming. This is how we can say that racist shaming circulates within institutions even though it is no longer related to the hyper-reflexivity of the surface of the body.

As Black women academics, we exist within racist contexts in which being made to feel shame, to be ashamed, makes us feel that institutionally we are abandoned by society as we are 'left to starve outside the boundaries of human kind' (Probyn, 2005: 3). This speaks total exclusion within the world of work, which makes us feel ashamed because we are affected by that shaming event instantiated by Whiteness as we come into contact with it (Ahmed, 2004). 'Coming into contact' with White-originated shame attempts to orient us to act in specific ways, to become ashamed, to feel shameful, to be filled with shame, as we feel the sting of tears and the heat in our faces when we know we have experienced racism, a racism of which our White colleagues seem to be (un)aware. Their being (un)aware relates to that knowing ignorance of racist injury to feelings, which keeps the world focused on White privilege (Mills, 1997; Yancy, 2008).

Further, White-originated Black woman shaming regulates behaviour and produces a relationality of self-awareness as we ourselves experience shame directly or feel vicarious shame because of the suffering of other women racialized as Black. These are aspects of 'the phenomenological experience of shame [in which] the self is both participant and watcher in its own' shaming event (Mokros, 1995: 1095) and in those of others, as we feel their shame, their shaming, as irrevocably ours. Pause here and think back to what you felt when you read the extract above. Go back and read it again. She is unknown to you but you felt connected to her in that moment of her shaming in a visceral way, as you sensed the injustice she was experiencing because it has also been your injustice or can potentially be your position in the future.

Her shaming interpellated her as 'ashamed', 'shamed' and 'shameful', as someone *affected* by shame, but as a reader of her extract, the impact of her shame is *affecting* (Ahmed, 2004). It is affecting, it affects us, because of our attachment to her as someone who has suffered because of racism, a suffering that we recognize. As a listener to her story, hearing her voice wobble with emotion, seeing her eyes well up as her voice grew thick with tears, I saw and heard the visible and audible impact of her shame as she recounted her story and transmitted this White-originated shame to me through the intensity conveyed in her voice and body (Brennan, 2004; Gutiérrez Rodríguez, 2010). This intensity was transmitted even while she was on the verge of tears, nearly losing it. My 'sensing' (Gutiérrez Rodríguez, 2010) her nearly losing it made me believe everything she told me in that moment, as I felt her shame.

How could we answer the question 'how do you feel?' in the face of such racist shame and shaming that affect us directly and vicariously? If we say we feel 'bad', 'ashamed', 'hurt', 'injured', would that lessen us as women? One of the things I have had to learn throughout my life is that I hurt, and to tell myself that this does not diminish me as a person but rather enhances my ability to analyse the world I inhabit. This analysis allows me to say, 'no, that shame I feel is really not about me at all but about that White racist person with whom I am interacting and about how they position themselves in the world'.

What I am saying through this is that we need to revisit and revise the image we have of ourselves as 'strong Black women', admit that 'Black does crack' and that there is nothing wrong with speaking as a survivor of and through racist hurt. To think through our feelings, to analyse and theorize racism through them rather than being immobilized by them because of fear that we are not strong enough, is already a show of strength. To admit that we need solidarity so as to survive the daily damage we experience at work already means that we are seeking to go beyond White-originated shame to build communities that matter much more, to knowledge and understanding that sustain our world view, ways of being in which we find comfort and socialities in which there is solace.

It is important to acknowledge that we hurt too, that we are brought to tears by our experiences of racism, that we take this home with us into our intimate lives and attempt to make sense of what we feel there. It is important to take back to the institution what we learn from our reflections so as to enable us to challenge the ruling image of 'the strong Black woman' that is part of institutional life. It is important to reveal the Black woman who feels the hurt caused by anti-Black woman racism in answer to the well-being agenda prevailing in universities, an agenda kept alive through staff well-being university-funded activities, such as lunchtime yoga and departmental well-being indices within the yearly planning cycle. What would happen if tackling racism became a part of well-being indices? It would be no less than a revolution in terms of a White supremacy that sees itself as entitled to the world it has created as well as its privileges, because its unmarked racial Whiteness designates that this entitlement should not be questioned (Mills, 1997).

To be a lone voice speaking about racism is to risk censure, especially if other Black people say that they have never experienced racism in their academic careers. To be so alone in your claim that racist injustice has occurred means your well-being is in your hands. This is because expecting an institutional response to racism that goes beyond the personal and looks at the institutional foundation for continuing racism would be to have a utopic vision of the Ivory Tower. 'Ivory is as ivory does' and the appellation speaks universities as White institutions in which anti-Black woman racism and its shaming events melt into thin air (Gordon, 1997). Their disappearance is to the White eye only, an eye that constantly has the Black woman academic body – individual, collective and epistemological – under surveillance for any sign of trouble, any possibility of a claim of racism to break the uneasy White conviviality of academia. Universities maintain themselves as White-only privilege panoptical zones, which exert governmentalities (Foucault,

1980) of silence and silencing to enable racist shaming events and Black women's shame to persist. Such silence and silencing of shame are inimical to Black women's well-being but are key to shame's unvoiceability regimes within UK HEIs.

Shame's unvoiceability regimes

Let us begin to think about shame's (un)voiceability with an example from my own experience many years ago.

> The programme leader was a White feminist. She wanted a White woman who was her friend to get the job that had been advertised. I disagreed and supported a more qualified and experienced Asian man over her friend, citing our responsibilities under equal opportunities legislation. She questioned my feminist credentials and asked me, 'what are you today, are you Black or a feminist?' She made it plain that the White woman would be hired because the course on which I also taught had already borne 'the brunt of employing Black people'. That brunt, of course, was me. The Asian man did not get the job, but he won his case at an industrial tribunal on grounds of racial discrimination. I was a witness on his behalf and, unlike the racist perpetrator, was not represented by university counsel. There was an internal investigation. I was spoken to by the head of department as part of the fact-find and this was audio-recorded so that no claims could be made afterwards that anything untoward had been said. I was summoned, questioned and verbally reprimanded by the vice chancellor for my disloyalty to the university. The White feminist, who walked around teary-eyed for months after the tribunal, was not reprimanded but rather pitied because of my betrayal and her public humiliation, though she kept her job until she retired. I, on the other hand, was put into a room with no windows, by myself, for two years so I 'would not experience victimization' and was 'sent to Coventry' in the department. I left the university to end my two-year stint in isolation, which makes me think that if I had stayed I could very well still be in that room.

I look at this now and think it is remarkable what we can survive and what we are asked to experience as Black women academics in contexts that see themselves as tolerant, as above racism. The White feminist could make her shame known through crying in public for several months but I was hidden in a room 'to protect me from victimization'. Wasn't the 'splendid isolation' of the room victimization in itself? Wasn't the room, in which I was isolated from departmental sociality, a location of shaming? It proclaimed, 'here is that woman who put anti-racist politics before us all as a department so she can't be trusted'. At that time, no one asked how I felt but the White feminist's feelings were constantly displayed on her tear-streaked face and her feelings were constantly being enquired about because of her public display of hurt.

My shame at her comments that Black people are a brunt to be borne, at the head of department's recording of our conversation lest I lied about it, at the vice chancellor's reprimand and disbelief as to the veracity of what I said about the event at the tribunal, and at being put in a room to separate me from my colleagues, was all unvoiceable within the department, though their shaming of me was loud and plain to see. The unvoiceability of my shame arose because it could not speak in a language that would be recognized or understood by the overwhelming White supremacy in which I was enclosed. This was because I was positioned as 'racialized other' and, as such, someone whose hurt feelings did not matter. Their approach to the legal requirement in race relations legislation to protect me from further victimization was to move me – and not the person who was found to have racially discriminated against the job applicant. This already shamed me into a space of unbelonging, both literally in terms of the room and psychically in terms of how I felt at the time.

Speaking today about how I felt then, I would describe myself as institutionally liminal. I went to work, did my job – but inside I remained frozen, cut off from my feelings the moment I entered the campus gates, lest they bubbled to the surface and my anger at being shamed emerged. I could never again harbour the hope, such as I'd had, that I would be recognized as an academic on equal terms with colleagues because of the excellence of my work. Instead, I had to remain vigilant for hurts that would threaten my personhood in order to refuse their shaming potential. My institutional liminality meant that I couldn't say I was being made to feel ashamed while the racist perpetrator was comforted by White sociality and her unquestioned place within it, even though her racism was publicly on show.

Claims of racism apparently do not cause White institutional or personal shame because these claims are easily erased as being caused by 'one rotten apple'. Or, in this case, shame was erased because the university denied that it was a zone of institutional racism and blame was attributed to me because I was a Black traitor who reported on a private conversation instead of playing by the institution's rules and keeping these egregious racist statements to myself. Yet how could I, as a Black woman who doesn't believe in standing by when injustice happens, possibly have done that? What is interesting here is how my reporting her racism became my problem, because I had made Whiteness vulnerable to shame and being shamed. I, therefore, had to bear the brunt of White shame at its own racism being outed instead of it being repressed as usual through institutional melancholia.

Melancholia is 'an affective state caused by the inability to assimilate a loss, and the consequent nagging return of the thing lost into psychic life' (Khanna, 2003: 16). The loss here is that of the racial innocence of the 'post-race' university and those who occupy it, when institutional racism and people's complicity in its operation are brought into the open, when the naked racism that operates within the 'post-race' Ivory Tower is laid bare. Institutions can be as racially melancholic as the people who occupy them, because people make up institutions, constructing them in their own image. So, time and again, we see the emergence of the White body, whether institutional or individual, as vulnerable to harm and requiring protection from the possibility of shame. The loss of racial innocence, allied with the construction of Whiteness as vulnerable, denies White hegemony and attempts to co-opt the body of the Black woman other – whether collective, individual or epistemological – as something that resists incorporation and so is problematic for the emergence of the desired 'post-race' White ego. As Anne Anlin Cheng (2001: 8) states, 'Freudian melancholia designates a chain of loss, denial and incorporation through which the ego is born.' The White ego, be it individual, collective or institutional, of necessity continually generates profound ambivalence around the loss of racial innocence and its accompanying racism that has been swallowed whole. Attachment to racism is problematized as inimical to collegiality and societally regressive, even though it is useful in maintaining the Racial Contract (Mills, 1997) that privileges those racialized as White. This problematization of racism moves to nostalgia for its certainties in terms of maintaining continuing White privilege, and to resentment at its troubling presence. As melancholic institutions, universities fixate on the possibility of racism, of what it might mean to have the finger of racism pointed at them. We see this melancholic attachment now in the uptake within UK HEIs of the White curriculum, and Black professor critiques as things that universities want to work on, much as we saw it in the past in equality and diversity practices, processes and cultures. Whites must avoid the shame of their own racism so racism continues to be melancholically repressed as part of shame's (un)voiceability regime. (Un)voiceability regimes ensure that universities are shorn of any meaningful engagement with race and racism through policies of de-racination that make race and racism 'cease to exist'. Race and racism are co-opted as part of mainstream institutional discourse, which relegates them to liminality through melancholic repression. Further, liminality is ensured by co-opting the demands of anti-racist social movements as universities' own policies and strategic goals. Deracination, melancholic repression of shame at racism and (un)voiceability regimes produce (un)liveable lives for Black women academics.

Shame, deracination and liveability

What is it to have 'a good life' as an academic in the context of shaming encounters where deracination means that universities become (un)liveable work contexts? What Judith Butler (2004) reminds us of is that injurability and aggression mean that vulnerability is differentially distributed across people. If as Black women we are liminal (Rollock, 2012) in organizations, at constant risk of shame, then we continue to have (un)liveable professional lives because of racism. How can I say racism, though, within the continuing insistence that we live in a 'post-race' society and racism is no longer relevant institutionally, societally or individually and its lack of relevance means that it no longer has any place in the curriculum? Those of us who work on race and racism will know what it is like to see this work diminished institutionally because it doesn't fit with prevailing deracinated epistemologies.

As is the case for knowledge, so it is for people. As Black women, we can no longer say that we experience racism because then we, in turn, will be called racists. Let me give you an example of what I mean from popular culture. In 2016, Jada Pinkett Smith publicly objected to the Whiteness of the Oscars, its racist exclusion of Black actors, and refused to attend the ceremony. In response, Charlotte Rampling chastized all those 'Black anti-White racists' who wanted to ruin the Oscars ceremony she was due to attend as a nominee. In common with White academics who think that Black people can be racist, the question is, in what world do they live?

They live in a world of their making. It is described by Eduardo Bonilla-Silva (2014) as a world in which there is racism without (White) racists, where racism can be denied and Black people can be shamed by the charge of anti-White racism. This again creates (un)liveable spaces of sociality in which Black women increasingly cannot voice injury to their feelings, the shame suffered because of White racism, because this racism is deniable. Deniability constantly returns racism to us, to our hyper-sensitivity, to us reacting negatively to 'just some long emails', to us needing to just get over it because it doesn't exist. (Un)liveability dictates that we continue to be within spaces of (un)location within which White skin means privilege and an institutional belonging that is never in doubt.

Conclusion

Our burden as Black women academics in White institutions is the Whiteness that is hegemonic, privileged and continually privileging itself while maintaining its self-proclaimed position as 'non-racist'. I use 'non-racist' rather than 'anti-racist' for a reason, because to be anti-racist still assumes the existence and significance of racism. 'Non-racist' is part of being 'post-race' – both are fallacious positions. However, they are the controlling matrix within which racist shame's (un)voiceability regime operates. Without the possibility of voice and recognition, racist shaming continues unabated within UK HEIs as a White strategy to contain Black women academics within their space of '(un)location'. What can be done about this, politically and personally?

As I said earlier, we should start saying 'I hurt' in answer to the well-being question and thereby challenge the institution. We can perhaps draw from Audre Lorde's ideas on anger as a foundation for Black feminist politics and apply these to racist shame's erotic life within institutions and without. In 'Uses of the erotic: The erotic as power', Lorde (2007) views the erotic as an untapped resource within us. Her 'erotic' is about the power contained in those feelings of ours that remain unrecognized and unvoiced. In Lorde's view, we need to take the first step in political action: recognition, so for our purposes that is recognizing our deep feelings of hurt from racist shaming. Doing so, we can begin being dissatisfied with our longstanding suffering, self-negation, numbness produced by racist shaming and act against this micro-aggression, speaking its name and impact. As we do this, we engage Lorde's 'erotic' because we begin the 'project of selfhood' as we see ourselves as coherent subjects. Voicing the location from where our shaming arises to show that we are not inherently shameful brings about our empowerment through affective transformation and the ending of our suffering (Musser, 2014). The erotic does not only reinforce individual subjectivity, it also enables the formation of Black feminist communities of mutual relationality (Musser, 2014). As a community of Black women academics, who are vulnerable to injury because of racist hetero-patriarchy, we must seek out the erotic and its solidarity politics because these are vital for the survival of the Black feminist community.

References

Ahmed, S. (2004) *The Cultural Politics of Emotion.* New York: Routledge.

Bhabha, H.K. (1994) *The Location of Culture.* London: Routledge.

Boden, D. (1994) *The Business of Talk: Organizations in action.* Cambridge: Polity Press.

Bonilla-Silva, E. (2014) *Racism without Racists: Color-blind racism and the persistence of racial inequality in America.* 4th ed. Lanham, MD: Rowman and Littlefield.

Brennan, T. (2004) *The Transmission of Affect.* Ithaca, NY: Cornell University Press.

Butler, J. (2004) *Precarious Life: The powers of mourning and violence.* London: Verso.

Cheng, A.A. (2001) *The Melancholy of Race: Psychoanalysis, assimilation, and hidden grief.* Oxford: Oxford University Press.

ECU (Equality Challenge Unit) (2015) *Equality in Higher Education: Statistical report 2015.* London: Equality Challenge Unit. Online. http://www.ecu.ac.uk/publications/equality-in-higher-education-statistical-report-2015 (accessed 7 September 2017).

Fanon, F. (1986) *Black Skin, White Masks.* London: Pluto Press.

Foucault, M. (1980) 'The eye of power'. In Foucault, M. *Power/Knowledge: Selected interviews and other writings, 1972–1977.* Ed. and trans. Gordon, C. Brighton: Harvester Press, 146–65.

Gilroy, P. (2004) *After Empire: Melancholia or convivial culture?* London: Routledge.

Goldberg, D.T. (2015) *Are We All Postracial Yet?* Cambridge: Polity Press.

Gordon, L.R. (1997) *Her Majesty's Other Children: Sketches of racism from a neocolonial age.* Lanham, MD: Rowman and Littlefield.

Gutiérrez Rodríguez, E. (2010) *Migration, Domestic Work and Affect: A decolonial approach on value and the feminization of labor.* New York: Routledge.

Khanna, R. (2003) *Dark Continents: Psychoanalysis and colonialism.* Durham, NC: Duke University Press.

Lorde, A. (2007) 'Uses of the erotic: The erotic as power'. In Lorde, A. *Sister Outsider: Essays and speeches.* Berkeley, Crossing Press, 53–9.

Mills, C.W. (1997) *The Racial Contract.* Ithaca, NY: Cornell University Press.

Mirza, H.S. (1997) 'Introduction: Mapping a genealogy of Black British feminism'. In Mirza, H.S. (ed.) *Black British Feminism: A reader.* London: Routledge, 1–28.

Mokros, H.B. (1995) 'Suicide and shame'. *American Behavioral Scientist*, 38 (8), 1091–103.

Musser, A.J. (2014) *Sensational Flesh: Race, power, and masochism.* New York: New York University Press.

Ngai, S. (2005) *Ugly Feelings.* Cambridge, MA: Harvard University Press.

Probyn, E. (2005) *Blush: Faces of shame.* Minneapolis: University of Minnesota Press.

Puwar, N. (2004) *Space Invaders: Race, gender and bodies out of place.* Oxford: Berg.

Rollock, N. (2012) 'The invisibility of race: Intersectional reflections on the liminal space of alterity'. *Race Ethnicity and Education*, 15 (1), 65–84.

Sedgwick, E.K. (2003) *Touching Feeling: Affect, pedagogy, performativity*. Durham, NC: Duke University Press.

Tate, S.A. (2014) 'Racial affective economies, disalienation and "race made ordinary"'. *Ethnic and Racial Studies*, 37 (13), 2475–90.

Yancy, G. (2008) *Black Bodies, White Gazes: The continuing significance of race*. Lanham, MD: Rowman and Littlefield.

Chapter 5

Inclusive ideals are not enough: Academia does not empower Black women

Ima Jackson

Introduction

This chapter focuses on the progressive ambitions and fantasies of a small newly evolving country, and the progressive ambitions and fantasies of a Black female academic – that's me. Although this story is set in Scotland, the themes of visibility and invisibility, insiders and outsiders, immigrants and emigrants are familiar, persistent and unwelcome features of the Black experience in academia and elsewhere (Collins, 2000). However, the relatively recent emergence of a new level of racial issues in Scotland, and the web of trying-to-be-inclusive intentions in which they take place, means that Scotland offers a novel perspective on that experience. Unfortunately, this story doesn't have a happy ending – not yet, anyway.

Scotland has generally considered itself a country of emigration, not immigration. It has exported colonists for hundreds of years: to the plantations in Ulster and the early colonies in America, and to the vast expanse of the British Empire in Africa and Asia, in which Scots played a disproportionately prominent part. Scots pride and nostalgia for that history has given way to a more thoughtful and realistic appraisal of Scottish colonial exploitation. Recently, for example, the importance of the slave trade to Scotland's economic development has been acknowledged by contemporary historians (Devine, 2011; Devine, 2015; Mullen, 2009).

Despite emigration dominating the national imagination, Scotland also experienced significant waves of immigration: from Scandinavia in the 8th to 15th centuries, from Ireland in the 19th century, and from Italy in the early 20th century. Although that European migration changed after the Second World War to immigration from South East Asia, Africa and the Caribbean, the numbers involved were a fraction of those experienced in England, so perhaps did little to disturb Scotland's sense of itself as a White, largely monocultural country (Brady, 2016; Meer, 2015).

'Alba' becomes Negra

As late as 1997, Scotland's minority ethnic population was just 1.1 per cent, compared with 7.2 per cent in England, and 32.4 per cent in Inner London. However, by the 2001 census, that figure had increased to 2.0 per cent, and it had doubled again to 4.0 per cent by 2011 (NRS, 2011). Such rapid changes in Scotland's ethnic composition emerged alongside huge political changes. Scots voted in favour of devolution in a 1997 referendum, and the first meeting of the new Scottish Parliament took place in 1999. With systems created to foster inclusion, openness and consensus, and with a Parliament elected by proportional representation, housed in a radical building designed by a Catalan architect, the new political settlement was optimistic and progressive. During this period, Glasgow took in a disproportionate number of refugees from Asia, Africa and the Balkans, further bolstering a national self-image of fairness and tolerance (Mooney and Scott, 2011; Scottish Government, 2016).

By 2011, 12 per cent of Glasgow's population had been born outside the UK (Vargas-Silva, 2013). While anti-migrant sentiment began to increase in some parts of England, polls reported that Scots held significantly more positive attitudes towards migrants than did their English compatriots, and migration itself was considered less of an issue in Scotland than elsewhere in the UK (McCollum *et al.*, 2014). It seems unlikely that these findings reflected inherently Scottish values. As the Scottish National Party (SNP) successfully increased its electoral popularity, it emphasized its desire to promote a political rather than an ethnic nationalism (Parekh, 2004). There are indications that this aspiration may have some grounding in reality. Scotland's first minority ethnic Member of the Scottish Parliament (MSP) Bashir Ahmad was SNP, and the nationalist party currently has one of only two minority ethnic MSPs, between them representing 1.6 per cent of the 129 members. Interestingly, several studies suggest that ethnic minorities in Scotland are more likely to identify as Scottish than British (CRER, 2011).

Migration became a key indicator of differentiation from Westminster policies. 'Take back control' was a slogan that influenced English voters to favour Brexit in the 2016 referendum (Hall, 2016). However, Scotland voted strongly in favour of remaining in the European Union, and the Scottish government sought enhanced powers to manage migration – by which they meant *increasing* the flow of migrants to Scotland. The image the Scottish government sought to promote was one of an outward-looking, internationalist nation, with a strong university and science sector (Sturgeon, 2016).

Scotland's distinctive attitude towards immigration in some way reflected Ahmed's findings (2007) relating to diversity, which showed that this term is used strategically by diversity practitioners in such a way that more easily supports existing organizational ideals or even denotes organizational pride, rather than issues of race and equality. In a similar way in Scotland and its institutions, engaging with migration and migrants is used as a way to demonstrate progressiveness and racial equality, but it is carefully controlled to distance itself from discrimination, and racial inequality embedded in that experience.

You'll have had your diversity, then?

I was a migrant too, of a modest kind, having moved to Scotland from England in the early 1990s. That would normally have been an unexceptional relocation, but as a Black woman I suddenly found myself much more visible than before. It was so rare back then for one Black person to see another in the street that we would greet each other with a friendly nod of recognition. Those glances and quiet smiles marked a discreet solidarity among the people of colour who had been born into or migrated towards Scotland and its Scottish Whiteness.

I pursued my career and started my family in an environment that was rapidly ethnically diversifying. One consequence of those demographic changes was pointed out to me recently by a Black Scottish colleague, when she joked that there are now *just too many* Black people in public spaces in Scotland's cities for us to give each other those wry, reassuring greetings that we once did. Scotland has reached a social and political tipping point, as ethnic diversity becomes more ordinary. Such change brings some paradoxes. An individual Black woman in an otherwise White society may be noticeable (personally visible), but she poses no threat to the status quo (i.e. is politically invisible and powerless). But when the same woman finds herself part of a rapidly growing Black and minority ethnic population, she becomes less visible as an individual, just as the Black demographic she now belongs to grows in visibility and in its potential for power.

The trajectory through visibility and invisibility towards hyper-visibility of women of colour was examined through the experience of Muslim migrant women by Ghorashi (2010) and it seems particularly relevant. Ghorashi (2010) demonstrated how migrant women in Holland had moved within public discourse from being largely invisible towards a hyper-visibility that focused on their perceived unemancipated selves as different from the emancipated Dutch women. Ultimately, this trajectory was further disempowering migrant women, rather than seeking to enable alliances, reduce isolation and increase their voice, as the increased visibility was purporting to do.

Patil and Purkayastha (2015) explored invisibility and hyper-visibility within mainstream media reportage of rape in the United States and India. They highlighted the relative invisibility of violence against women of colour in the United States and the hyper-visibility of women from elsewhere (in this case India) which, they argued, leads to a perpetuation of a civilization narrative that has been maintained post-colonially and that impacts directly on collective memory about sexual assault, space and race.

I mention these explorations of visibility, invisibility and hyper-visibility in public narratives to highlight the differing mechanisms through which the experience of women of colour becomes located and held. Mirza (2009) explores how the visibility/invisibility experiences of Black women within universities are finely tuned to the needs of the organizations and hence often used to demonstrate diversity and globalization at the expense of actually engaging with the marginalization that occurs within the organizations.

In some regions of Britain, power through numbers may be slowly increasing, but in Scottish academia, the numbers are vanishingly low. In 2010, 1 per cent of staff identified as Black, 2.4 per cent as 'other' (including mixed heritage) and, with the inclusion of Asian staff, the total number of Black and minority ethnic academics in Scotland was 1,645 out of 16,855 (HESA, 2011). As a Black academic, I find myself working in a particularly unwelcome situation where high visibility is combined with low influence. I remain conspicuous among a cohort of academics who are, almost without exception, White; my sense is that while diversity is formally recognized and ostensibly valued, when genuine differences in perspective and understanding are highlighted, they are not always understood or even recognized as of value.

It's not easy to judge the extent of your own visibility and influence when you don't have other colleagues to share your experiences with. That is especially the case in universities, which are usually smart enough to conceal evidence of overt prejudice or discrimination. But we know that racism has recently been not just present but that it has an influence on many Black and minority ethnic people's careers. I trained as a nurse and then a midwife, before completing a PhD and leaving the profession. There is plenty of evidence of racism from Black and migrant nurses, who repeatedly – and independently – report on being de-skilled and discriminated against, and on the lack of recognition and of promotion by their lecturers and employers, as well as the attitudes of patients and their relatives (Allan,

2010; Buchan, 2003; Glover, 2013; Henry, 2007; Jones and Snow, 2010; Likupe, 2006).

I was to uncover my own direct evidence of prejudice, as I describe shortly. But first a personal anecdote: a modest epiphany that marked for me both difference, and an unexpected solidarity. It was a Wednesday afternoon in March. I walked quickly through the city streets, noticing (albeit no longer greeting) other Black people. I was on my way to a rare university 'school development session' in a luxury hotel in the city centre. I was accompanied by a White colleague I'd recently met and liked very much. My promotion had been rejected two days previously. I wasn't particularly noticing or thinking about any of this, until I found myself standing at the doorway of the large conference hall where we were to meet. I found that I physically couldn't take the next step to walk into the room. The space was full of White people, sitting at the large round tables or standing chatting in small groups. I hadn't meant to voice my thoughts, but I found myself exclaiming 'Oh gosh it's just so White!' My new friend was startled by this, and responded promptly: 'I'd never think like that.' A few words each: but in that brief exchange we had each unexpectedly expressed the truth as we saw it. We looked at each other in surprise, as this sudden candour recast our relationship. The uneasiness left between us was caused in some way by me raising the issue of colour. By saying it out loud I had created the issue, brought it into being. If I hadn't said anything, there wouldn't have been a problem. In a blog post, Ahmed discusses the difficulties of naming the sexist and racist experiences women encounter and suggests that 'words can allow us to get closer to our own experiences; words can allow us to comprehend what we experience after the event … [but] to give the problem a name can be experienced as magnifying the problem; allowing something to acquire a social and physical density' (Ahmed, 2014).

I noticed that there was one other brown face in the room, a man I had never met. Nonetheless, he noticed me too and came over to introduce himself. There was a moment when the three of us stood together and just regarded the room, trying to puzzle out what had just happened. Such moments have been described as 'micro-aggressions', but in this case, perhaps 'micro-intensities' would be more accurate. The poet Claudia Rankine uses a quote from Zora Neale Hurston to describe such scenarios in her book *Citizen*: 'I feel most colored when I am thrown against a sharp white background' (Rankine, 2014).

Why had I responded with such physical resistance to the meeting? I presume a range of reasons must be in play. I was still hurt at being rejected for promotion; I clearly felt highly visible and exposed in that setting. As

Mirza (2014–15) suggests, for post-colonial women of colour there is an ever-present negotiation between and within our daily social experiences and that understanding perhaps encapsulates some of that moment. But I've experienced and managed those issues without difficulty before. I think the physical layout of the room contributed to the intensity of the moment. The cabaret-style tables were meant to facilitate discussion, engagement and new ideas, free of the social and institutional structures that usually inhibit such creative thinking. The kind of creative reflection, in other words, that universities were created to generate. But I didn't see a room energized by a fresh group dynamic. I saw a White monoculture that perceived me as different. I hesitated to cross the threshold, because I suddenly lacked the intellectual and emotional energy to make that okay for my colleagues, the people, as Ta-Nehisi Coates says, 'who think of themselves as White' (Coates, 2015).

Mirza (2014–15) writes of this effort and the cost to individual Black women. She references Simmonds (1997: 227), who describes being in the Whiteness of academia like a fresh water fish swimming in sea water, to highlight the embodied intersectionality within the Black 'othered' woman's struggle over the defining materiality of her educational experience. Mirza believes that Simmonds provides a powerful account of the 'personal costs of marginality for Black women and the profound experiences you have when moving between "worlds" of difference in higher education' (Mirza, 2014–15: 2).

Puwar (2004) developed the idea of a 'racial somatic norm' to explain some of the mechanisms through which Black bodies are fashioned and held in place when they do not characterize the norm within White institutions. Mirza expands on this when she describes the 'disorientation, a double take as you enter a room, as if you are not supposed to be there. You are noticed and it is uncomfortable' (Mirza, 2014–15: 7). As Puwar explains:

> Social spaces are not blank and open for any body to occupy. Over time, through processes of historical sedimentation, certain types of bodies are designated as being the 'natural' occupants of specific spaces ... Some bodies have the right to belong in certain locations, while others are marked out as trespassers who are in accordance with how both spaces and bodies are imagined, politically, historically and conceptually circumscribed as being 'out of place'.
>
> (Puwar, 2004: 51)

However, it is the understanding offered by Sara Ahmed that reflects most accurately my experience in Scotland, when she suggests that if we get used to inhabiting Whiteness in institutions or spaces 'it can be a survival strategy to learn not to see it, to learn not to see how you are not reflected back by what is around' (Ahmed, 2012: 35). I was not prepared; my usual mechanisms were not in place to protect and deflect the unwelcome experiences away from myself.

Liberté, égalité, Beyoncé

What do you do when you have no Black colleagues? You make some. My PhD was a qualitative study that examined the institutional mechanisms that distribute power and manage the social frames in which midwives and pregnant women negotiate their places in the obstetric system of care. My findings suggested that midwives had little awareness or insight into these constructs, despite the huge impact they had on their practice. I found this intellectually stimulating, but professionally depressing. I quit midwifery, and took up a new post which (I realize now) also entailed understanding the mechanisms of professional exclusion.

I was fortunate to be appointed the lead for a university-hosted project that aimed to support the adaptation of refugee and asylum-seeking and latterly all migrant health professionals to professional life in Scotland. In my new post, I developed a national accreditation process through which asylum-seekers and other migrants could be helped to have the qualifications and experience that they had acquired in their home countries recognized and adapted so they could pursue their professional careers in Scotland (Jackson, 2005). I found myself newly at ease with an unexpected group: the very Black and minority ethnic refugees and migrants who were in the process of transforming Scotland's demographic. They were also challenging some of the stories and assumptions about Scotland's so-called 'tolerance', as we were about to discover together. I was there to help them, as a UK-born Black guide and vanguard. While delighted to be working with this inspiring group of people, I was also ambivalent about the risk of becoming pigeon-holed because I was supporting a marginalized and vulnerable group. I did not want to become limited to that institutional role or category. As Ahmed (2012) forewarned, I did not want to be the race person – and as Shilliam suggests:

> The hyper-visibility that comes with being in a department where
> you are the only Black and Minority ethnic academic might make
> you feel far too vulnerable to voice any concerns about race and

> racism. It is not uncommon, for example, for Black and minority
> ethnic academics to avoid taking part in 'race groups'. Indeed,
> you might be worried that to be associated with a race would
> tend to de-professionalise you in the eyes of your colleagues.
>
> (Shilliam, 2014)

My concerns were realistic. Immigration was a huge social change for
Scotland, and was becoming the topic of serious academic inquiry among
my White colleagues – but it was more than that. It was as though if
others pronounced on, for example, the legal, medical or social impacts of
migration in Scotland, speaking into the pre-existing spaces they already
occupied, it was greeted with greater recognition and prestige. Whereas my
academic focus often required new spaces to be created, because it came
from the reality of people's migrant experience of the academy and policy,
so was somehow positioned as less relevant. Initially, I thought this was
about migration itself but then came to realize it was also about me as a
Black woman speaking with authority about experiences of migration. I
was a category error. I did not belong.

This field should have offered the same opportunities for me: a career
route to maintain my interests in policy, social justice and institutional
change, while exploring their relationship with race and equalities issues.
But the institutional frame in which I was held by my university made it
almost impossible to maintain the academic distance required for that kind
of work. I wanted to explore race and equalities issues, but in the process,
became something of a race and equalities issue myself. As Shilliam says,
'Black academics are always Black, and it is not necessarily by choice'
(Shilliam, 2014). From my point of view, my Black British identity gave me
some (limited, but valuable) insight into the experience of Black migrants in
a White country. But I knew my experience was not theirs.

Yet the university found it hard to maintain such distinctions. I led a
small team, among whom I was the only Black person. We were successful in
our work, gaining local and national recognition. We campaigned with some
success against the 'othering' and stigmatization of refugees. Yet, despite
being born and raised in the UK and working for years in the National
Health Service (NHS), a few months of engagement with refugees had been
sufficient to mark me as 'other' in the eyes of the institutions I worked with.
My British identity became enmeshed with that of the refugees. For example,
colleagues would speak about protecting 'our' NHS and 'our' patients, as if
those things were not equally 'mine'. I was positioned as personally bringing
in 'these people' to the country, as if migration had been *my* choice and

doing. My own dismay and distress at this exclusion did at least give me some perspective on the immeasurably greater challenges faced by migrants. Although my situation was very secure by comparison with their exposure in society, we nonetheless had a kind of emotional bond that I found very moving. The people I worked with who were seeking refuge and asylum impressed me with their professionalism, determination and resilience. But beyond that, I felt a kind of acceptance and understanding in their presence. Mine was no longer the only Black female face in my department: as lead for a refugee project in a White institution, I was enabling people of colour with diverse backgrounds to inhabit the corridors of the Ivory Tower. I had sought and found my own kind of asylum among the asylum-seekers.

I write these words with a kind of wary irony, since I know how privileged I am; because I am proud of the innovative work we accomplished together, and because I remain a grateful friend with some of the refugees I worked to support. But – and here I feel a sharp conflict between my different identities – while those refugees would support me in whatever way they could, they could not help me in my career. In fact, they probably held me back, since my professional association with the new migrants that Scotland had so proudly welcomed also became an association with powerful racist tropes, including the 'impoverished African', the 'fake refugee', 'illegals' and 'welfare scroungers'. Such ideas were as embedded in the institution as they were in society more widely.

A university is usually too smart an organization to express such views directly. But recognizing that they are nonetheless held is not to succumb to discrimination-induced paranoia. As it became clear that the development of the project and progress in my career were both being obstructed, I began taking careful notes in meetings with management and administration. Professional colleagues from a range of organizations, including my university, made statements about refugees that included the following:

'I mean they want everything for nothing … they are just so demanding. They are saying that they should just be given everything. It is just ridiculous – we shall have to be careful or they will ask for too much.'

'Well you have to be really careful … you know they already try and cheat loads – we don't want to make it any easier for them.'

'We will have to get the department to undersign the risk of the project. I have already talked about this with finance and they are not happy for this money just to be spent on the refugees without some sort of guarantee that the money will come … even if it is NHS Education the money is coming from and they are a regular client.'

The university, perhaps like Scotland, recognized the 'brand appeal' of diversity, not least because they were pursuing a commercial strategy of internationalization. But it felt as though they also wanted migrants and migration impact confined, and I – with my dark skin and my headscarf – was the perfect person to negotiate and safely manage those boundaries. As I listened to professional voices discuss the othering of the migrants, it was impossible not to speculate about what equivalent thinking or speaking might be going on about me. Although patches of colour might be appearing on campus, it seemed that the White hegemony of the Ivory Tower would remain untouched. I too was kept outside. Like the refugees, I found I had to be smarter, work harder and act Whiter for my skills to be accepted. Yet while the refugees recognized their need for professional adaptation to their new situation, I came to resent the additional efforts required of me. Why was my situation so different from those of my White colleagues? Why did I have to force my body to enter that conference room? Why was I the only one keeping quiet notes of the prejudice manifest in meetings? If any adaptation was needed, I thought, it was for the university to *adapt to me* and my Black and minority ethnic colleagues.

As a Black female academic in Scotland, it has taken me rather a long time to understand what that actually means in practice. I kept thinking that my experience was atypical, rare or confined to Scotland: but now I realize just how prevalent it is in other places. I had imagined that if I were an academic in law or in business, my experience would have been different. But I was wrong about that. The space I occupy is exactly the same space that is given to many Black female academics (Alexander and Arday, 2015). My understanding of my own experience in academia has been changed by social media – the interest and support garnered by engaging with others nationally through Black British Academics and across Europe. The Women of Colour conference in Edinburgh in 2016 (Emejulu, 2016) added to this, with a dawning realization of how perfectly typical the narrative of my journey has been.

I feel that I will have had a successful career if, by the end of it, I am working with Black colleagues, that we are enabled to focus with support, and that the institution respects the work – in a real sense. bell hooks (1991) suggests that, as Black feminists, we have to theorize from a place of pain. I respect that point of view as much as I resent it. Academia should welcome diverse voices, but institutional prejudice, inertia and self-interest mean that the intellectual energy that could so readily be tapped still remains largely hidden.

Writing my own experience in the context of wider Black feminist theory helps me realize that my personal struggle was shared by many others. I had thought that by sheer force of effort I could compel my university to change. It's hard to realize in your fifties that that has not happened. Nonetheless, I cannot give up.

References

Ahmed, S. (2007) 'The language of diversity'. *Ethnic and Racial Studies*, 30 (2), 235–56.

— (2012) *On Being Included: Racism and diversity in institutional life*. Durham, NC: Duke University Press.

— (2014) 'Problems with names'. *Feminist Killjoys*, 25 April. Online. https://feministkilljoys.com/2014/04/25/problems-with-names (accessed 16 March 2017).

Alexander, C. and Arday, J. (eds) (2015) *Aiming Higher: Race, inequality and diversity in the academy*. London: Runnymede Trust. Online. www.runnymedetrust.org/uploads/Aiming%20Higher.pdf (accessed 8 March 2017).

Allan, H. (2010) 'Mentoring overseas nurses: Barriers to effective and non-discriminatory mentoring practices'. *Nursing Ethics*, 17 (5), 603–13.

Brady, J. (2016) 'Names reveal Dundee's become multi-cultural'. *Dundee Evening Telegraph*, 27 December. Online. www.eveningtelegraph.co.uk/fp/names-reveal-dundees-become-multi-cultural (accessed 29 July 2017).

Buchan, J. (2003) *Here to Stay? International nurses in the UK*. London: Royal College of Nursing.

Coates, T.-N. (2015) *Between the World and Me*. New York: Random House.

Collins, P.H. (2000) *Black Feminist Thought: Knowledge, consciousness, and the politics of empowerment*. 2nd ed. New York: Routledge.

CRER (Coalition for Racial Equality and Rights) (2011) *Scottish Identity and Black and Minority Ethnic Communities in Scotland: An introductory review of literature*. Glasgow: Coalition for Racial Equality and Rights.

Devine, T.M. (2011) *To the Ends of the Earth: Scotland's global diaspora, 1750–2010*. Washington, DC: Smithsonian Books.

— (2015) *Recovering Scotland's Slavery Past : The Caribbean connection*. Edinburgh: Edinburgh University Press.

Emejulu, A. (2016) '2016 Conference: Black Feminism, Womanism, and the Politics of Women of Colour in Europe'. Online. https://woceuropeconference.wordpress.com/2016-conference (accessed 10 March 2017).

Ghorashi, H. (2010) 'From absolute invisibility to extreme visibility: Emancipation trajectory of migrant women in the Netherlands'. *Feminist Review*, 94 (1), 75–92.

Glover, J. (2013) *Impact Assessment Summary Report: Nursing Career Opportunities Project*. Edinburgh: NHS Lothian. Online. www.nhslothian. scot.nhs.uk/YourRights/EqualityDiversity/ImpactAssessment/Rapid Impact Assessments/Nursing Progression Project EQIA Jan 13.pdf (accessed 27 February 2017).

Hall, M. (2016) 'Boris Johnson urges Brits to vote Brexit to "take back control"'. *Daily Express*, 20 June. Online. www.express.co.uk/news/politics/681706/Boris-Johnson-vote-Brexit-take-back-control (accessed 20 March 2017).

Henry, L. (2007) 'Institutionalized disadvantage: Older Ghanaian nurses' and midwives' reflections on career progression and stagnation in the NHS'. *Journal of Clinical Nursing*, 16 (12), 2196–203.

HESA (Higher Education Statistics Agency) (2011) 'Staff in higher education institutions 2009/10'. Online. www.hesa.ac.uk/news/03-03-2011/higher-education-staff (accessed 10 March 2017).

hooks, b. (1991) *Yearning: Race, gender, and cultural politics*. London: Turnaround.

Jackson, I. (2005) *Adaptation of Asylum Seeker and Refugee Nurses: Glasgow overseas professionals into practice*. Glasgow.

Jones, E.L. and Snow, S.J. (2010) *Against the Odds: Black and minority ethnic clinicians and Manchester, 1948 to 2009*. Manchester: Manchester NHS Primary Care Trust, in association with the Centre for the History of Science, Technology and Medicine, University of Manchester.

Likupe, G. (2006) 'Experiences of African nurses in the UK National Health Service: A literature review'. *Journal of Clinical Nursing*, 15 (10), 1213–20.

McCollum, D., Nowok, B. and Tindal, S. (2014) 'Public attitudes towards migration in Scotland: Exceptionality and possible policy implications'. *Scottish Affairs*, 23 (1), 79–102.

Meer, N. (2015) 'Looking up in Scotland? Multinationalism, multiculturalism and political elites'. *Ethnic and Racial Studies*, 38 (9),1477–96.

Mirza, H.S. (2009) *Race, Gender and Educational Desire: Why black women succeed and fail*. London: Routledge.

— (2014–15) 'Decolonizing higher education: Black feminism and the intersectionality of race and gender'. *Journal of Feminist Scholarship*, 7–8, 1–12.

Mooney, G. and Scott, G. (2011) 'Social justice, social welfare and devolution: Nationalism and social policy making in Scotland'. *Poverty and Public Policy*, 3 (4), Article 5, 1–21.

Mullen, S. (2009) *It Wisnae Us: The truth about Glasgow and slavery*. Edinburgh: Royal Incorporation of Architects in Scotland.

NRS (National Records of Scotland) (2011) *NRS Business Plan: 2011–12*. Edinburgh: National Records of Scotland. Online. www.nrscotland.gov.uk/files/about-us/nrs-business-plan-2011-12.pdf (accessed 29 July 2017).

Parekh, B. (2004) *Realising the Vision: Progress and further challenges: The Report of the Commission on the Future of Multi-Ethnic Britain (2000) revisited in 2004*. London: Runnymede Trust. Online. www.runnymedetrust.org/uploads/publications/pdfs/RealisingTheVision.pdf (accessed 9 March 2017).

Patil, V. and Purkayastha, B. (2015) 'Sexual violence, race and media (in)visibility: Intersectional complexities in a transnational frame'. *Societies*, 5 (3), 598–617.

Puwar, N. (2004) *Space Invaders: Race, gender and bodies out of place.* Oxford: Berg.

Rankine, C. (2014) *Citizen: An American lyric.* Minneapolis, MN: Graywolf Press.

Scottish Government (2016) *A Plan for Scotland: The Government's programme for Scotland, 2016–17*. Edinburgh: Scottish Government. Online. https:// beta.gov.scot/publications/plan-scotland-scottish-governments-programme-scotland-2016-17/documents/00505210.pdf?inline=true (accessed 29 July 2017).

Shilliam, R. (2014) 'Black academia in Britain'. *The Disorder Of Things*, 28 July. Online. https://thedisorderofthings.com/2014/07/28/black-academia-in-britain (accessed 8 March 2017).

Simmonds, F.N. (1997) 'My body, myself: How does a Black woman do sociology?'. In Mirza, H.S. (ed.) *Black British Feminism: A reader*. London: Routledge, 226–39.

Sturgeon, N. (2016) 'In full: Nicola Sturgeon's post-Brexit speech to the IPPR'. *The Scotsman*, 25 July. Online. www.scotsman.com/news/in-full-nicola-sturgeon-s-post-brexit-speech-to-the-ippr-1-4185993 (accessed 10 March 2017).

Vargas-Silva, C. (2013) 'Migrants in Scotland: An overview'. Migration Observatory briefing, 18 September. Online. www.migrationobservatory.ox.ac. uk/resources/briefings/migrants-in-scotland-an-overview (accessed 20 March 2017).

Chapter 6

Reflecting on a journey: Positionality, marginality and the outsider-within

Claudia Bernard

Introduction

In this chapter, I reflect on my journey in the academy by discussing some of my experiences and the challenges I have faced. I examine themes of positionality, marginality and the outsider-within status through the lens of Black feminism, to show how these factors framed my journey in the academy, and specifically how they influenced the development of my scholarship. I begin with a brief overview of the ways in which my background as a social worker had influenced my development as a scholar. I elaborate on the ways in which Black feminist thinking helped me to inhabit a space in the academy, before going on to consider the critical role of mentoring in that development. In the final section of the chapter, I discuss the development of my theoretical approach, using my book *Constructing Lived Experiences* (Bernard, 2001) as illustration.

How my social work background informed my theoretical orientation

I begin with my social work background and its undoubted influence on my development as an academic. As a social work scholar, my primary research area has been to develop Black feminist-centred research into child abuse and neglect, and gender-based violence, with a particular focus on Black families. In my research, I have thus been concerned to explore the roles of gender, race and class in framing encounters with welfare services. My interest in these topics derives largely from my experience as a social worker during the late 1980s and early 1990s. I was continually brought face-to-face with the destructive consequences of structural inequalities. As the International Federation of Social Workers declares: every day social workers are working with life at its extremes, witnessing the highs and lows of human capabilities and behaviour (IASSW *et al.*, 2014). Social work is a highly gendered profession; it is largely women working in the field and the majority of service users are women. During my time as a social worker, I bore witness to manifestations of patriarchy in terms of gender role socialization, the violence women and children in the family experience, and the gender dynamics that underlie much child protection social work.

A feminist social work lens enabled me to decipher how gender relations played out in the organizations and fostered the mother-blaming discourse that prevailed, so that social workers placed blame on women when they couldn't protect their children from being subjected to factors beyond their control, such as poverty, racism, domestic violence and poor social housing (Krane *et al.*, 2013). But most importantly, I bore witness to the devastating impact of neoliberal policy and its role in the demonization of those who experience multiple disadvantages, portraying them as undeserving, at best, and fuelling the blame-the-victim approach that prevails in welfare discourse. Observing in practice the disregard of the way that racism shapes the everyday realities of Black people enabled me to better understand how Black children come to be over-represented in the care system, and Black adults, men in particular, in the mental health system. Thus, my experiences as a social worker highlighted the importance of understanding that social work practice must engage with the issues that lie at the root of social injustice, namely the inequality and social divisions that exist in our society.

All this made me think again about the evidential bases of many social work interventions with Black families, and this acted as a spur later to create new knowledge areas to make visible 'the voices that are not heard, the voices that are wounded and/or oppressed' (hooks, 1989: 7). In this way, I was drawn to take a social justice perspective that is open to interrogating the role of the state and social work in particular, when working with marginalized and oppressed people. These experiences and observations significantly influenced the areas of inquiry and the questions I examined in my research. I therefore came to the academy with the goal of creating alternative epistemologies to explore how marginalized and oppressed groups make sense of their experiences in ways that enable them to represent the truths of their lived realities in the context of societal racism.

Outsider-within the academy

As a Black woman inhabiting intersecting identities in the academy, I was confronted with several challenges, mainly involving alienation, isolation and marginalization. Black feminist thinking and critical race theory (CRT) provided me with some tools to help navigate my way through what at times has been a very 'chilly climate' (Britton, 2017). Put simply, Black feminism affirms that Black women's multiple social locations produce specific understandings of their racialized, gendered and class-based positions in societies where these dimensions are significant markers of experience. Specifically, CRT enables us to see the insidious ways in which racism impacts on social structures, practices and discourses (Yosso, 2005: 70; Rollock, 2012). These two distinct but overlapping frameworks have been significant in the development of my pedagogical approach, as well as in developing my own Black feminist perspective. At the beginning of my academic journey, I drew heavily on Patricia Hill Collins (2004) to help with creating a sense-making approach to my experiences. Collins uses the 'outsider-within status' to call attention to the difficulties that Black female scholars face in reconciling their personal experiences, identities, values and perspectives with those that dominate academia.

Black feminist thinkers recognize that racial micro-aggression is an invisible feature of Black scholars' experiences in the academy (Carter-Black, 2008; Daniel, 2009; Davis *et al.*, 2011–12; Trotman and Greene, 2013; Vakalahi and Hardin Starks, 2010). Specifically, the insights from Black feminist scholars such as Collins gave me new tools for thinking about the racial micro-aggressions that are regular occurrences in the academy; the commonplace verbal and behavioural racial slights that marked me as other, subtly communicated that I did not belong, and relegated me to a subordinate status (Rollock, 2012). I am reminded of the numerous occasions during my career where I have been mistaken for a student, secretary or administrator. So I use 'I thought you were … fill in the blanks' as a metaphor to capture these incidents of misrecognition. This misrecognition clearly positions me as an outsider (Henderson *et al.*, 2010; Turner, 2002).

Making sense of the nuances underlying misrecognition requires insights into the subtleties of racial micro-aggression. Only then can we understand how I was positioned in the academy. Ostensibly, Black feminist insights helped me to cultivate strategies to inhabit the White space of the academy, in situations where I simultaneously felt both hyper-visible and invisible. As Lewis and Simpson point out, in Acker (2012: 14): 'overly visible as exceptions and invisible as marginalised'. Essentially, it was important to interrogate the ways in which race-constructed otherness becomes inscribed and played out to identify how such elements have informed the development of my Black feminist standpoint. Yet at the same time, the terrains I encountered helped me to crystallize the notion that being on the margins in the academy gave me a unique angle of vision on self, the academy and society (Collins, 1990; hooks, 1989). The work of

Black feminist scholars, such as Collins, and other feminist race scholars, such as bell hooks (1989), Audre Lorde (1984), Kimberlé Crenshaw (1994) and Heidi Safia Mirza (1995), laid the foundation for me to develop a counter-narrative to challenge the assumption that Western and Eurocentric forms of knowledge are the only valid ways of knowing. So in the realm of knowledge creation, hard questions needed asking about subjugated knowledge, such as whose knowledge counts and whose gets left out (Yosso, 2005). Black feminist thinking helped me to counter the dominant narratives about Black people in social work.

Thus, I drew my primary inspiration from Black feminist perspectives and insights in order to make creative use of my marginality and outsider-within status to create new and different perspectives about multiple-oppressed communities. Taking a Black feminist standpoint afforded me an overall explanatory framework for interrogating racialized gendered issues in social work practice.

Mentoring as a tool of resistance

Perhaps not surprisingly, it became apparent early in my career that I needed to carve out spaces to develop the tools needed to navigate the intricate and complex racialized and gendered encounters I faced in my academic development. This led me to seek mentoring as a means of self-development. In my early career, I was the sole Black academic in my team, while there were few Black women academics in senior positions in the academy, and therefore little chance of finding a same-race/same-gender mentor. It is telling, though, that it was not until mid-career that I felt able to ask my institution to provide the funds to employ the services of a Black mentor, external to the academy. By this time, I was confident of my academic standing; I had held many departmental positions of responsibility, and was sitting on various university committees. Moreover, as a scholar in a research-intensive university, I was also confident that my research was making a strong contribution to the scholarly literature on social work, thus my request felt justified.

Even so, I had to make a strong case to my heads of department as to why, in the absence of a supportive atmosphere, I needed to work with a mentor who shared a similar background to me, and therefore would understand some of the obstacles created by race- and gender-based discrimination, in striving to achieve academic advancement. As a result, I had the good fortune to work with two excellent professional Black feminist coaches, which critically assisted with my optimal development. It is important to note, however, that on the two occasions I was able to access the resources to find mentors from outside the academy, I had heads of department who were sympathetic to the issues concerned. In contrast, I have had eight heads of department during my time in this academy, the majority of whom were indifferent to my aspirations, with one or two being particularly hostile to my advancement. This has made me acutely aware of the role that unconscious bias can play in the career progression of Black academics.

Mentoring played an immensely important role in my efforts to succeed in an academic environment that was at times indifferent or hostile. To some degree, the mentoring relationships set the frame for me to understand the salient issues and supported me in significant ways. First, they gave me thinking space to identify, recognize and disentangle what Bhopal (2016) refers to as the covert, subtle and nuanced racism in the White space of the academy. Second, they gave me the tools to work creatively with what Alleyne (2005) refers to as 'invisible injuries' that we as Black people experience in workplace environments. Third, having a safe space to express myself authentically and talk about racial battle fatigue (Smith, 2004) enhanced my ability to voice my visceral feelings to make sense of the subtle and covert signifiers for the 'other' in the academy. As hooks (1994: 74) states, we theorize from pain and struggle to 'recover and remember ourselves'. Moreover, the mentoring helped me to make sense of what Acker (2012: 11) has described as 'the emotional work of controlling one's own feelings and the public expression of them'. I am referring to the emotional work involved in ensuring that we do not dissociate from our true selves in order to tolerate being in the academy. As Trotman and Greene (2013) and Wilder and colleagues (2013) rightly argue, we Black women have to work twice as hard if we are to survive and achieve any success in the academy.

Although I consider myself to be someone who is strong and resilient, I was forever mindful of the powerful cultural messages about the 'strong Black woman', which I believe can hinder us from talking about our vulnerabilities and drawing truthful insights from our experiences. The mentoring gave me a space in which to express my vulnerabilities and my rage, and heightened my recognition of my internal coping mechanisms and emotional responses to the difficulties I encountered in the academy. This process was not only empowering, but also gave me the energy and momentum to maintain hope and optimism.

Drawing on Yosso's cultural wealth model (2005) provided a framework to make sense of my experiences to enable me to operate in an environment where sexism and racism can intensify problems for Black female academics. The key components of Yosso's model I employed were, notably, the ideas of aspirational, navigational and resistance capital. Yosso's aspirational capital refers to the hopes, dreams and aspirations we may have despite persistent inequities; her navigational capital is concerned with the skills and attributes needed to navigate an unsupportive and toxic academic environment; and resistance capital refers to the experiences of Black communities in engaging with social justice issues to secure equal rights and collective freedom. A key tenet of Yosso's notion of cultural wealth is the centrality of the experiences, talents and skills Black people bring with us to the academy.

I used mentoring as a form of resistance (Henderson *et al.*, 2010), as it helps me to nurture my emotional resources and maintain a positive view of myself in an environment where my self-esteem is continually undermined (Chesney-Lind *et al.*, 2006; Davis *et al.*, 2011–12). In short, looking back now, I recognize the value of having the mentors I did because they enabled me to use key facets of cultural capital to negotiate the academic milieu in which I am situated. This is particularly important because it encouraged me not to downplay the significance of my scholarship and, vitally, allowed me to consider how to stop an unsupportive environment from holding me back.

That said, as I reflect back on my experiences, I am reminded that I was frequently unsure about how my scholarship would be valued by the promotion and reward committees in the academy. I was acutely aware when pursuing promotion that the academy has an organizational culture dominated by White middle-class men, and I was mindful of the suggestions that there can be a devaluing of work, which is race-related (Turner, 2002). Many scholars (for example, Henderson *et al.*, 2010; Jackson and Johnson, 2011; Thomas and Hollenshead, 2001) have commented that Black female academics are more likely to report that their scholarship is less valued compared with White men and women, and with Black men. Recognizing that, as an outsider in the academy, I had to confront the realities of the power structures in its networks was a key learning point for me.

Fast forward to 2014 when, on my promotion to professor, one of my White colleagues remarked, 'You have now reached the top of your game – you are part of the elite group now.' Few would dispute that professorial rank brings with it a certain set of privileges. At the same time, it is important to understand that there are complexities involved in simultaneously occupying both a privileged and a disadvantaged position, which is how I feel I am positioned in the academy because of being socially marginalized. My sense is that, although respect and recognition are proffered to professors, the continued racial micro-aggression reminds me of how deeply ingrained racial stereotypes are and how they manifest in unconscious ways.

Crucially, Black feminist thinking and critical race theory were key sources of insight and inspiration, which helped me to make sense of my journey. As a Black feminist scholar working in a predominantly White, male-dominated environment, I found that the lenses of Black feminism helped to crystallize how we have to be constantly shifting our positioning to adjust to the race- and gender-based inequalities we navigate in the academy (Jean-Marie and Brooks, 2011; Hall and Sandler, 1982; Harris, 2016). Black feminist thinking provided a critical framework for me to make sense of my realities in the academy. A Black feminist theoretical approach not only helped me to better understand the specificities of my experiences, but it also enabled me to develop an oppositional discourse of the experiences of marginalized and oppressed groups. Especially important is that I brought my lived experience as a Black woman, a social worker and a researcher together to create new knowledge about Black women's oppression and resistance in my book *Constructing Lived Experiences* (Bernard, 2001). The book is a good example of this oppositional discourse. In the next section, I discuss how a frame of Black feminist thinking helped me to develop the research that formed the basis for the book.

The development of a Black feminist approach to childhood sexual abuse in Black families

My research has played a significant role in bringing attention to childhood sexual abuse in Black families that face multiple oppressions. Grappling with my own experiences of race and gender dynamics in the academy has helped me to develop a paradigm grounded in an understanding of gendered power relationships within Black families. My book (Bernard, 2001) on childhood sexual abuse develops the idea of divided loyalty to explore the implications for Black mothers' help-seeking and protective strategies. Specifically, I use the concept of divided loyalty to unravel the emotional and behavioural responses of Black mothers. In particular, the effects of the abuse on the mothers' parenting are posited to analyse the ways in which their mothering roles are impacted by the aftermath of abuse. Because I elucidate how mothers have to come to grips with the societal racism that constructs their parenting to be deficient, while at the same time grappling with complex gendered power relations in their families, the book offers a new perspective and expands our understanding of the effects of child sexual abuse in Black families.

With this Black feminist approach, the book examines the web of relations in which meaning is constructed for Black mothers. I was especially attuned to a feminist audience, but was conscious that I needed also to reach those who might not be sensitive or sympathetic to a feminist approach but nonetheless have to intervene in Black families to secure the safety of their children. My analysis provided insights and stressed the importance of the roles of gender, race and power in influencing how Black mothers perceive their concerns and priorities. I used margins as a metaphor to critique much feminist writing on mothers in discourses about child sexual abuse and illustrated my argument with examples from the data.

The assumption underlying my approach in the book is that Black women's perspectives are always on the margins of feminist analysis – never at the centre. Writing this contribution for a text that advanced an explicitly feminist agenda gave me the creative and intellectual space to develop a Black feminist piece for putting forward an alternative perspective that not only illuminates the misconceptions and mother-blaming discourse that permeates social work practice but, most importantly, also exposes the contradictions that exist for Black mothers.

Conclusion

In this chapter, I have highlighted issues I confronted on my academic journey and the effect of my background as a social worker on the direction of my scholarship. Writing this chapter has evoked for me how my social work background laid a rich foundation for the development of the theoretical orientation that framed my research. It significantly influenced the questions I sought to interrogate. My social work background made me well placed to address and give voice to the lived experiences of Black children in their families, and it strengthened my resolve to do the kind of research that would have practical benefits for Black families in the child welfare system, as well as to advancing knowledge of the subject.

The mentoring I received undoubtedly proved valuable to my academic journey, as it gave me a particular kind of sustenance. I now recognize the significance of mentoring in providing the support and affirmation that helped me garner my emotional resources to develop positive strategies for coping against the odds in a frequently hostile environment. More to the point, mentoring was emancipatory as it helped me to build resilience and illuminated ways for me to navigate the barriers that are largely invisible in the academy. Looking back now, I can see other benefits of mentoring: the opportunities it gave me to elucidate what were complex, multi-layered, racialized and gendered experiences that were tightly interlinked. In short, having this kind of space to think through the issues of the outsider-within positionality has been hugely beneficial to my academic success. Fundamentally, the mentoring relationships helped me to harness my strengths to affirm my authority as a scholar and to be confident that what I had to say was important. For Black female academics in predominantly White institutions, mentoring is vital if they are to be successful in their academic careers. To borrow from Cheryl Wall (1991: 1–2): 'The position or place we are assigned on the margins of the academy informs but does not determine the positions or stance we take.'

References

Acker, S. (2012) 'Chairing and caring: Gendered dimensions of leadership in academe'. *Gender and Education*, 24 (4), 411–28.

Alleyne, A. (2005) 'Invisible injuries and silent witnesses: The shadow of racial oppression in workplace contexts'. *Psychodynamic Practice*, 11 (3), 283–99.

Bernard, C. (2001) *Constructing Lived Experiences: Representations of black mothers in child sexual abuse discourses*. Aldershot: Ashgate.

Bhopal, K. (2016) *The Experiences of Black and Minority Ethnic Academics: A comparative study of the unequal academy*. London: Routledge.

Britton, D.M. (2017) 'Beyond the chilly climate: The salience of gender in women's academic careers'. *Gender and Society*, 31 (1), 5–27.

Carter-Black, J. (2008) 'A black woman's journey into a predominately white academic world'. *Affilia: Journal of Women and Social Work*, 23 (2), 112–22.

Chesney-Lind, M., Okamoto, S.K. and Irwin, K. (2006) 'Thoughts on feminist mentoring: Experiences of faculty members from two generations in the academy'. *Critical Criminology*, 14 (1), 1–21.

Collins, P.H. (1990) *Black Feminist Thought: Knowledge, consciousness, and the politics of empowerment*. New York: Routledge.

— (2004) 'Learning from the outsider within: The sociological significance of black feminist thought'. In Harding, S. (ed.) *The Feminist Standpoint Theory Reader: Intellectual and political controversies*. New York: Routledge, 103–26.

Crenshaw, K.W. (1994) 'Mapping the margins: Intersectionality, identity politics, and violence against women of color'. In Fineman, M.A. and Mykitiuk, R. (eds) *The Public Nature of Private Violence: The discovery of domestic abuse*. New York: Routledge, 93–118.

Daniel, J. (2009) 'African-American women's journey to academia and their experiences as occupational therapy professors'. *McNair Scholars Research Journal*, 2 (1), 49–66.

Davis, D.J., Chaney, C., Edwards, L., Thompson-Rogers, G.K. and Gines, K.T. (2011–12) 'Academe as extreme sport: Black women, faculty development, and networking'. *Negro Educational Review*, 62–3 (1–4), 167–87.

Hall, R.M. and Sandler, B.R. (1982) *The Classroom Climate: A chilly one for women?* Washington, DC: Project on the Status and Education of Women. Online. http://eric.ed.gov/PDFS/ED215628.pdf (accessed 13 October 2017).

Harris, T.M. (2016) '"It takes a village to raise a professor": Being mentored and mentoring from a marginalized space'. In Tassie, K.E. and Brown Givens, S.M. (eds) *Women of Color Navigating Mentoring Relationships: Critical examinations*. Lanham, MD: Lexington Books, 41–59.

Henderson, T.L., Hunter, A.G. and Hildreth, G.J. (2010) 'Outsiders within the academy: Strategies for resistance and mentoring African American women'. *Michigan Family Review*, 14 (1), 28–41.

hooks, b. (1989) *Talking Back: Thinking feminist, thinking black*. London: Sheba Feminist Publishers.

— (1994) *Teaching to Transgress: Education as the practice of freedom*. New York: Routledge.

IASSW (International Association of Schools of Social Work), ICSW (International Council on Social Welfare) and IFSW (International Federation of Social Workers) (2014) 'Global Agenda for Social Work and Social Development: First report – promoting social and economic equalities'. *International Social Work*, 57 (4), Supplement, 3–16.

Jackson, S. and Johnson III, R.G. (eds) (2011) *The Black Professoriat: Negotiating a habitable space in the academy*. New York: Peter Lang Publishing.

Jean-Marie, G. and Brooks, J.S. (2011) 'Mentoring and supportive networks for women of color in academe'. In Jean-Marie, G. and Lloyd-Jones, B. (eds) *Women of Color in Higher Education: Changing directions and new perspectives* (Diversity in Higher Education 10). Bingley: Emerald Group Publishing, 91–108.

Krane, J., Strega, S. and Carlton, R. (2013) '"G-d couldn't be everywhere so he created mothers": The impossible mandate of maternal protection in child welfare'. In Strega, S., Krane, J., Lapierre, S., Richardson, C. and Carlton, R. (eds) *Failure to Protect: Moving beyond gendered responses*. Halifax, NS: Fernwood Publishing, 11–29.

Lorde, A. (1984) *Sister Outsider: Essays and speeches*. Freedom, CA: Crossing Press.

Mirza, H.S. (1995) 'Black women in higher education: Defining a space/finding a place. In Morley, L. and Walsh, V. (eds) *Feminist Academics: Creative agents for change*. London: Taylor and Francis, 145–55.

Rollock, N. (2012) 'Unspoken rules of engagement: Navigating racial microaggressions in the academic terrain'. *International Journal of Qualitative Studies in Education*, 25 (5), 517–32.

Smith, W.A. (2004) 'Black faculty coping with racial battle fatigue: The campus racial climate in a post-civil rights era'. In Cleveland, D. (ed.) *A Long Way To Go: Conversations about race by African American faculty and graduate students*. New York: Peter Lang, 171–90.

Thomas, G.D. and Hollenshead, C. (2001) 'Resisting from the margins: The coping strategies of black women and other women of color faculty members at a research university'. *Journal of Negro Education*, 70 (3), 166–75.

Trotman, F. and Greene, B. (2013) 'Women of color in academia'. In Comas-Díaz, L. and Greene, B. (eds) *Psychological Health of Women of Color: Intersections, challenges, and opportunities*. Santa Barbara, CA: Praeger, 287–302.

Turner, C.S.V. (2002) 'Women of color in academe: Living with multiple marginality'. *Journal of Higher Education*, 73 (1), 74–93.

Vakalahi, H.F.O and Hardin Starks, S. (2010) 'The complexities of becoming visible: Reflecting on the stories of women of color as social work educators'. *Affilia: Journal of Women and Social Work*, 25 (2), 110–22.

Wall, C.A. (1991) 'Introduction: Taking positions and changing words'. In Wall, C.A. (ed.) *Changing Our Own Words: Essays on criticism, theory, and writing by black women*. New Brunswick, NJ: Rutgers University Press, 1–15.

Wilder, J.A., Jones, T.B. and Osborne-Lampkin, L. (2013) 'A profile of black women in the 21st century academy: Still learning from the "outsider-within"'. *Journal of Research Initiatives*, 1 (1), 27–38.

Yosso, T.J. (2005) 'Whose culture has capital? A critical race theory discussion of community cultural wealth'. *Race Ethnicity and Education*, 8 (1), 69–91.

Chapter 7

The struggle to find a voice on Black women's health: From the personal to the political

Jenny Douglas

Introduction

This chapter aims to document my journey as a Black female academic who has witnessed and experienced racism in public health, first through my mother's and aunt's experiences in the National Health Service (NHS) and then when I myself was working in health promotion and public health. Factors influencing health have motivated all my degree choices: my first degree, my master's degree topic and my PhD research. This brings me to my current role as an early career researcher, who happens to be in her sixties, trying to address the gaps in research on Black women's health, so that Black women can live the long and healthy lives we deserve.

The female members of my family had a tradition of working as nurses in the NHS. Their personal experiences of racism in the NHS and the experiences they witnessed of other Black people in the Service made me more aware and sensitive to Black women's raced and gendered experiences. I became motivated to focus on Black women's raced and gendered experiences in the context of health. This chapter examines issues around race, gender and health and the importance for Black women of building a support network. Despite the fact that many Black women have fought and worked for better health services for Black and minority ethnic women, their families and communities, this activism is seldom acknowledged or documented. The chapter takes a Black feminist perspective, challenging the invisibility of Black women in health research and seeking to render the health behaviour and experiences of Black women more visible.

My academic journey

My academic journey was partly driven by my ethnicity. I am African-Caribbean, born in Wolverhampton to African-Caribbean migrants from Jamaica. Like many people of their generation who migrated from Jamaica in the 1950s and 1960s, my parents were in search of a better life for themselves and their children (Chamberlain, 2006; Goulbourne, 2002; James,1993). Caribbean parenting practices were closely related to the educational aspirations they had for their children, encouraging further and higher education. They saw educational achievement as a means of achieving social mobility (Barn *et al.*, 2006).

My father arrived in 1951 and my mother followed in 1953. They married shortly after my mother arrived. To some extent, my mother's experience was similar to that of the character Hortense in *Small Island* (Levy, 2004), as my mother hardly knew my father when she arrived in the UK. She had been a teacher in a primary school in Jamaica but her qualifications were not recognized in England and she was advised that, if she wanted to train as a teacher she would have to start by taking O levels. She did not work outside of the home until after her youngest child had gone to school, so she took it upon herself to teach me (the oldest of five) and my siblings before we went to school. I was, therefore, able to read and write when I went to nursery school aged 3. My experience at primary school was very different from those reported by many researchers (e.g. Coard, 1971; Stone, 1981) as I was encouraged and supported to learn and achieve academically. I took my 11-plus exam at the age of 10 and went to the grammar school of the borough in which we lived. This was what my parents and wider family expected – no other possibility was even considered. At this point in my journey, I did not realize that my experience at primary school cut at right angles with that of many other Black children growing up in a British inner city in the 1960s. Research on education at this time portrayed African-Caribbean young people as under-achievers, regarded by teachers as culturally and intellectually inferior (Stone, 1981). Early research on the experiences of young children of Caribbean parents demonstrated the low expectations for them held by teachers and the siphoning of young Black children into units for children deemed 'educationally subnormal' (Coard, 1971).

However, I was the only Black child in the grammar school for the seven years I was there. During this time, my academic aspirations were thwarted and by the time I came to do my A levels, my teachers had convinced me that the best I could aim for was to be a nurse. My parents, like many Caribbean families, had decided that despite their hardships, the educational opportunities for their children would be better in the UK than in the Caribbean. They held the British educational system in high esteem and expected their children to do well. My mother had by this time started training to be a nurse and midwife (taking her O levels at the same time as I took mine). All of my aunts who had come from Jamaica were nurses. My mother expected me to do better than she had done and there was always an assumption that I would go to university. She convinced me not to do nursing but to study for an academic degree at a university.

My mother and aunts experienced racism and discrimination in the NHS even though they had trained as state-registered nurses (SRNs) rather than state-enrolled nurses (SENs). Black women were often discriminated against within the NHS and directed towards training as SENs rather than SRNs (Beishon *et al.*, 1995; Fog Olwig, 2012). This restricted their career development and progression as the SRN qualification was required before one could be a midwife, health visitor or senior nurse manager. First subconsciously and then very consciously, I became aware of my mother's and aunt's day-to-day experiences of oppression and racism as Black women working within the NHS. It was not only their own experiences that my family discussed, but also those of other Black people who were treated badly by doctors and nurses and denied access to much-needed healthcare. This angered me and instilled in me a desire to be in a position to address these racial inequalities in health provision.

I do not recall encountering direct, overt discrimination at school, though I was very aware that some of my teachers assumed that I was not as academically able as my White peers, although I achieved good grades in my eight O levels. Although I was in the science stream, taking three science A levels, there was an unspoken assumption that I would not go to university to undertake an academic course but would pursue a nursing career like the other women in my family, so possible academic courses were never discussed with me. I applied to universities offering degrees in nursing – pioneers at the time: Manchester, Liverpool and Kings College London.

However, I decided not to go to university to pursue a nursing degree but to spend another year at a further education college to improve my A-level grades and explore other university courses. Here, I met other Black students aiming to go to university and was introduced to Black feminist literature. A major influence on my own political development and awareness during the 1970s was, without a doubt, the civil rights movement in the United States. I followed with interest and excitement the developments in the Black Power movement, the Black Panthers, the Soledad Brothers,

Angela Davis, Eldridge Cleaver, Huey P. Newton and Martin Luther King. I listened to and drew upon the debates around community action, anti-racist and anti-discriminatory strategies. It was here that I developed my awareness and understanding of racism and its implications for Black people primarily in the UK and the US, but also globally and in the context of colonialism and imperialism.

Angela Davis, in particular, influenced and interested me. I followed her trial and subsequent acquittal. My early engagement with her work was focused on her prison and trial experience, the experience of other political prisoners, the prisons and Black liberation (Davis, 1971, 1974). The interaction between the theoretical strands of race, class and gender and the embryonic basis of intersectionality were explored in her later work and I developed my understanding of the impact and ways in which racism, sexism and classism interlocked in the lives of Black women over the following years (Davis, 1982, 1990).

I went to university to undertake a degree in microbiology and virology, as this was related to health and disease. It was then that I became interested in public health and would have welcomed the opportunity to pursue further academic work in this area had the option been available. The academic discipline of public health in 1976 was far more alive and well in the US than in the UK. It was while studying for a master's degree in environmental pollution control that I became more aware of social, economic and political factors affecting health and realized that the promotion of health did not depend purely on technological factors and expert knowledge, but also on social, economic and political factors. I realized that people had little say in the policymaking process and were powerless to influence political decisions on topics related to health and the environment. Environmental issues related to Black communities had not yet become prominent in the UK. The Flint water crisis in the United States, when the water supply became toxic to residents in a predominantly African-American area as a result of cost-cutting measures, demonstrates the importance of environmental issues for Black communities. Following my master's degree, I continued this area of research to examine policies aimed at reducing lead in the environment (Collingridge and Douglas, 1984). There was little public awareness that lead pollution would disproportionately affect young Black children in inner-city areas. They tended to reside in old properties with lead pipes and lead paint, in inner-city streets that had high levels of motor traffic that used lead-based petrol. However, environmental issues were not the focus of campaigns by Black communities in the UK.

Theory to practice, practice to theory

While continuing to research lead pollution, I also became involved with a number of Black community development organizations in Handsworth, Birmingham. Their main objective was to build support for Black people in the area, and they were working to effect change and give local people a say in local plans and initiatives, as well as lobbying statutory organizations around issues of racial discrimination and equality (Cottle, 1978; Bryan *et al.*, 1985). They focused on (mainly men in) the criminal justice system, discrimination in housing, health services and social welfare. I became involved in initiatives ranging from housing to education, the legal system and care of under-5s. While developing appropriate adult literacy approaches for African-Caribbean adults, I became familiar with the work of Paulo Freire (1972), and the political importance of language and the ways of using the teaching of literacy to develop social, political and economic awareness and 'conscientization'. Freire's approach to teaching literacy was to use people's day-to-day experiences and raise awareness of inequalities in areas such as access to health services.

My focus on health and community development began through my involvement with a Black women's project in the 1980s: Handsworth Young Mothers' Project. My involvement with Black women's projects crystallized my theoretical perspectives with regards to race, class and gender. The establishment of Birmingham Black Women's Group and the other Black women's organizations afforded me the opportunity to discuss my experiences of oppression together with other Black women, and made me realize that I was not alone in the view that feminism, as projected and articulated by predominantly White middle-class women, appeared to have little relevance to the lives and experiences of Black women (Amos and Parmar, 1984). The theoretical flaws in second-wave feminism with respect to its relevance for Black women are of particular importance in relation to community development and health. Working with local Black women, I learnt first-hand about their experiences of health and health services that were important to them, such as the misuse of Depo-Provera – the injectable contraceptive (Brent Community Health Council, 1981), the racist attitude of NHS doctors and nurses (Bryan *et al.*, 1985), lack of appropriate food and dietary advice, inappropriate maternity services (Larbie, 1985), and lack of appropriate mental health services and services for sickle cell and thalassaemia disorders (to name a few).

Between 1982 and 1984, I worked as a research and development officer for Training in Health and Race (THR), a project funded by the

Health Education Council and administered by the National Extension College. This project was partly a response to the emerging racial inequalities in health. Its aim was to set up and run training courses for NHS workers to help them work more effectively to meet the needs of Black and minority ethnic communities, as well as to support community initiatives organized around health. Although THR was not a statutory organization, it was initially viewed by some community health initiatives with suspicion and an expectation that it would hijack, rather than support, community health initiatives. Many community health projects were dependent upon short-term funding, as was THR. During this project, I became involved in a number of national initiatives and also learnt the limitations of cultural awareness training for health workers. I recognized the need to develop an understanding among health workers of the causes of inequalities in health and the role played by racism and poverty in the health experiences and health outcomes of Black communities and specifically Black women. It was while working with this project that I realized the importance of assuming a role where I had more influence in public health.

In 1984, I took up a permanent post as a health promotion manager with a health authority, setting up and developing a health promotion department. Here I had responsibility for developing health promotion and public health programmes in an area of Birmingham. A major influence on my theoretical development was the opportunity to visit the Caribbean during the tenure of a travelling fellowship to examine approaches to health and nutrition education in Jamaica, Barbados and Trinidad (Douglas, 1987). It was here that I was introduced to the work of the World Health Organization and the 'Health for All' strategy (WHO, 1985). 'Health for All' principles informed the work and approaches of local health promotion units, and were based upon notions of community development, community participation, and empowerment. I was able to develop a number of health promotion programmes and initiatives, which I developed further in my role as director of health promotion, my next post in the NHS. My theoretical perspectives were based on the key principles of the Ottawa Charter for Health Promotion (WHO, 1986), identifying the issues local people believed were important to their health. This involved undertaking research to ascertain health concerns before developing health promotion programmes (Douglas, 1995, 1996).

In this role, I was able to obtain external funding for several research and development initiatives on the health needs of Black and minority ethnic communities (Douglas, 1997). As well as my full-time post, I now had two small children and had embarked on a master's degree in sociological research in healthcare. I realized that, while my first degree and master's were relevant and useful for my work in health promotion and public health, I was becoming more aware that social and economic factors, such as poverty, work and housing, had as much – if not more – influence on health than biological and genetic factors. As a Black female senior manager in the NHS, I experienced racism and discrimination and often felt under greater scrutiny than my White male peers. This discrimination expressed itself often in the form of my seniors withholding information from me that I needed to be able to fulfil my role, and not accepting my authority and legitimacy as a senior manager. In some instances, my White male deputy colluded with this behaviour, attending meetings on my behalf but without my knowledge. Needless to say, there were no promotion or developmental opportunities – a situation well documented by other authors (Liff and Dale, 1994; Davidson, 1997). There were few other Black female senior managers.

Based on my previous community work with Black women and health, I wanted to explore the health experiences of Black women more systematically. As part of my master's degree, I undertook research on the health of Black women, comparing those working in the NHS with Black women employed elsewhere. The findings from this study identified the higher prevalence of fibroids, breast cancer and lupus among Black women compared with other groups, such as White women. It was clear that race, gender and class influenced the lives of Black women and hence their health (Douglas, 1991), but still I had not made the theoretical leap to naming 'intersectionality' or applying it to my health promotion and public health work.

Becoming and being an academic

At this stage, notions of intersectionality, as articulated by Kimberlé Crenshaw (1989), underpinned my community development work, while my developing work in health promotion and public health was a separate trajectory, although I had a clear understanding that Black women's health was affected by housing, employment and family life. Speaking at a conference at Spelman College in 1987 about the health of Black women in the United States, Angela Davis stated:

> But we have become cognizant of the urgency of contextualizing Black women's health in relation to prevailing political conditions. While our health is undeniably assaulted by the natural forces beyond our control all too often the enemies of

our physical and emotional well-being are social and political.
That is why we must strive to understand the complex politics of
Black women's health.

(Davis, 1994: 55)

Although I used approaches developed with reference to Black feminists
such as Angela Davis in my community development work, in my paid
work in health promotion and public health I did not think a Black feminist
approach was valued, as mainstream public health work – both medical and
clinical – was still very male-dominated. I also kept the two strands of my
practice quite separate. At this stage in my intellectual journey, I felt that I
had to dichotomize these two approaches. In my community development
work I felt comfortable using Black feminist perspectives, but in the NHS
policy environment I felt I had to work within a different paradigm and
couldn't see that a Black feminist perspective was easily transferable to
public health and health promotion.

Health promotion and new public health theories at this time
promoted community development through the principles of the Ottawa
Charter for Health Promotion (WHO, 1986), which incorporated a critical
approach to public health and focused on inequalities in a general sense, but
did not engage with the specific inequalities as they play out in relation to
the lives of Black women. It was only during the conceptualization of my
PhD research that I was able to bring intersectionality to my understanding
of health promotion and public health so the two strands came together in
a meaningful way. First, I wanted to bring a Black feminist methodology to
my research.

My focus was cigarette smoking by young Black women (Douglas,
2014). Earlier research on smoking among young women linked cigarette
smoking to material disadvantage. As Black women in inner cities were
more likely to experience material disadvantage, we might expect them to
have higher levels of cigarette smoking. However, this was not the case.
This was because earlier research on young women and smoking had only
considered age, gender and class and had not utilized an intersectional
framework incorporating race, gender, age, class and culture. My awareness
began to crystallize when I was developing a conceptual framework to
analyse and understand my PhD findings in context and I realized that these
two paradigms – intersectionality and public health – were not mutually
exclusive, but could and should be placed in conversation with each other.
Once this insight became apparent, I was able to exploit and develop the
heuristic value of this convergence. The heuristic advantage secured by the

theoretical integration of Black feminist and health promotion perspectives was relevant to health promotion and public health more widely.

Bowleg (2012) argues that, in public health research, issues of race, gender and class are often explored separately rather than by developing frameworks and methodologies to examine the multiple and interlocking effects of racism, sexism and classism. I began to realize that these perspectives needed to be brought together in order to develop a more nuanced and informed perspective on the experience of Black women, which I discuss later in this chapter. This has been more widely recognized by scholars writing about intersectionality and health (Mullings, 2000; Schulz and Mullings, 2006). As a Black researcher researching Black women's health, I had to operate initially within a field of intellectual discourse and activities where the needs and concerns of Black women were erased. So it becomes imperative for Black intellectuals to redefine, reconstruct and reconceptualize the terms within which these debates are conducted (Bowleg, 2012; Davis, 1990; Schulz and Mullings, 2006).

By 1995, the NHS was undergoing perpetual reorganization and I wanted to pursue an academic career so I could undertake research on Black women and health. I had a mistaken notion that it would be easier to combine full-time work and bringing up a young family with undertaking a part-time PhD. I was successful in obtaining a lectureship at a university close to home, albeit on a short-term, three-year contract. This made it easier to look after my two children and take them to school, and the university had a nursery and ran sports schemes in the long summer holidays. Although I was a lecturer, the department had a 5* rating in the Research Assessment Exercise and I was expected to publish, submit research proposals, and coordinate a European research project. My study had to take a back seat and I spent many years registering for my PhD, then suspending it because of the pressure of work. My notion of having more time to complete a PhD in an academic environment was totally unfounded. However, I often felt that, without a PhD, I had little chance of progressing to senior lecturer. Racism and discrimination were rife in the university and manifested in a range of ways, from exclusion to micro-aggressions to quite direct racism. For example, a male member of staff dressed up as a Black and White Minstrel at a staff Christmas party!

My lived experience as a Black female academic has played out in a multi-layered way. Contingently, there were times when I experienced support and appreciation within the academic workplace, but I was also on the receiving end of racialized bullying and harassment. The latter found expression in over-surveillance, micro-management and a refusal to recognize and acknowledge my contribution to teaching, research and other activities that my academic role encompasses. One of the ways in which racism and discrimination operate in the academy is to 'keep you busy' – often on low-level work no one else wants to do (Jones, 2006). A second way is presuming that you are incompetent (Gutiérrez y Muhs *et al.*, 2012; Jones, 2006). This means you are spending time and energy proving your competence rather than writing research papers and proposals. This, plus restrictions on attending academic conferences and meetings, prevents obtaining the requirements for promotion. Furthermore, the lack of mentoring of Black academics means that no one discusses the unwritten rules of the institution in relation to promotion.

When you are one of a small group of Black colleagues working in a White-dominated institution, the temptation to individualize such experiences can be immense. However, during my professional journey, I have been able to engage with literature that addresses these issues, and also to discuss my experiences with Black academics who work in other institutions and who are part of a range of Black networks within which I am embedded (Oyewumi, 2003). As a consequence, I was able to grasp the fact that my experiences could not be individualized and had to be understood as the expression of a phenomenon that shapes the working lives of Black intellectuals within the academy (Burke *et al.*, 2000; Mirza, 2006; Wright *et al.*, 2007).

As my three-year contract was coming to an end, I successfully applied for a senior lectureship. This time, it was at a university some distance from my home. As a senior lecturer, I was able to bring together all aspects of my previous academic training and experience, which included a good understanding of public health practice, research and theory. However, racism and discrimination expressed itself in a number of different ways. Some of the White lecturers questioned my academic credentials (Jones, 2006), because my appointment was as a senior lecturer.

Again, I was determined to complete my PhD, but it was difficult to find the time to focus on it. There were two other Black women in my faculty who were both trying to complete PhDs and for a time we formed a PhD peer support group. The group worked well initially; we shared useful resources, arranged training sessions together and gave each other support and motivation (Gregory, 1999).

The completion of my PhD is an object lesson for women like myself, who are already mature students in a full-time job and have young children when they start postgraduate research. We may well feel that it is too difficult to undertake a PhD while working full time. In my case, it was confounded by repeated periods of ill health. Unlike students who are Research Council funded and do their PhD full time over three or four years, I had to fit my research into a life that was already overflowing with commitments and responsibilities. This left little time for my research and it took me longer to complete my PhD part time, and I was even older than I had planned when it was finished.

In March 2008, I had another major health issue – a severe stroke. Although initially devastating, the period of recovery from the stroke gave me the time to review my life and my priorities for the future. My experience of another serious health condition made me more determined than ever to address inequalities in the population's health. I was determined to focus on the political imperatives of reducing the inequalities in health faced by Black women. Once I was fit to return to academic work and study, I felt a renewed sense of purpose and enthusiasm and managed to combine my part-time PhD study with recovering my physical and psychological strength and re-entering the academic workplace. I also learnt to put my own health first, as Black women so seldom do.

Although there has been some research on women undertaking PhDs and the difficulties of combining higher study with work and home life, there is scant research on the experiences of Black women academics who do so, particularly part time. It was helpful to read some of the published work in this field, for example Cole and Gunter (2010), which gave me inspiration, purpose and hope – particularly the chapter in which Heidi Safia Mirza discusses her academic journey. Although little is published on the PhD journey of Black students in the UK, there is more literature about the experience of African-Americans in the United States (Green and Scott, 2003).

My later narrative is no different from that of many African-Caribbean women, and indeed other women, who study part time while working and bringing up a family. However, Black women also have to deal with racism and discrimination. For me, it was difficult undertaking a PhD while working full time and, during my period of study, I went through significant life changes. However, my thinking matured over time and I was able to draw on public health, health promotion and women's studies and explore the relevance of intersectionality to health promotion and public health.

My PhD is an analysis of cigarette smoking among young African-Caribbean women in the mid-2000s. I was prompted by my work as a health promotion practitioner in public health during the 1990s, when a major issue in public health was cigarette smoking among young people and young women in particular. I worked in areas where there were sizeable Black and minority ethnic populations of young people and could find no public health research on young African-Caribbean women and cigarette smoking, despite the discourse about the link between cigarette smoking and disadvantage. If such a link existed, then we would expect to see more African-Caribbean than White young women to be smoking. I wanted to investigate whether this was indeed the case.

As my study looked at African-Caribbean women, identity and cigarette smoking, I drew on the emergent body of literature on young African-Caribbean women and identity by Black feminist theorists in the UK, including Mirza (1992), Phoenix (1988), Reynolds (2002) and Wright and others (2007). This literature challenged the way in which traditional (White) feminist research and scholarship had either rendered Black women invisible or perpetuated negative stereotypes and representations of young Black women. Black feminist scholars in the 1980s developed their own standpoint and drew attention to the ethnocentric and biased assumptions of classic gender analysis (Anthias and Yuval-Davis, 1983; Brah, 1992; Carby, 1982; hooks, 1982). Amos and Parmar (1984) critiqued the homogenizing and universalizing approach of White feminist scholarship which, in attempting to define the oppression of women, failed to acknowledge the specificity of the experience of Black and minority ethnic women. As bell hooks contended:

> The force that allows White feminist authors to make no reference to racial identity in their books about 'women' that are in actuality about White women is the same one that would compel any author writing exclusively on Black women to refer explicitly to their racial identity. That force is racism. In a racially imperialist nation such as ours, it is the dominant race that reserves for itself the luxury of dismissing racial identity while the oppressed race is made daily aware of their racial identity. It is the dominant race that can make it seem that their experience is representative.
>
> (hooks, 1982: 138)

The development of Black feminisms has spawned a significant literature, which reflects the distinctive nature and commonalities of Black British feminists (Mirza, 1997; Young, 2000), African-American feminists (Boyce Davies, 2006), African feminists (Mekgwe, 2006) and Caribbean feminists (Barriteau, 2006; Reddock, 2007). Research informed by Black feminist perspectives on young Black women and social identity was directly relevant to my PhD study. Black feminism is concerned with power relations, racialized boundaries and the lived realities of Black women. Intersectionality theory was developed by African-American legal scholar Kimberlé Crenshaw (1989) in response to the second-wave feminism that privileged gender but paid little attention to 'race' or ethnicity. Bowleg (2012) defines intersectionality as:

> A theoretical framework for understanding how multiple social identities such as race, gender, sexual orientation, SES [socioeconomic status] and disability intersect at the micro level of individual experience to reflect interlocking systems of privilege and oppression (i.e., racism, sexism, heterosexism, classism) at the macro social-structural level.
>
> (Bowleg, 2012: 1,267)

In the 25 years since Crenshaw (1989) coined the term 'intersectionality', both Black feminism and intersectionality have become widely recognized in disciplines such as sociology and social policy, but the concepts are fairly new to health and social care, particularly nursing, public health and health promotion. When exploring and researching the health of African-Caribbean women, researchers should adopt an intersectional approach that places Black women at its centre. Biomedical and epidemiological research does not always take account of the social, cultural and political context of the lives of Black women.

Since obtaining my PhD, I have focused my academic research on the health of Black women. With a group of other Black women academics, I have established a Black Women's Health and Wellbeing Research Network, which holds regular conferences (Douglas and Watson, 2013) and seminars in order to bring together the disparate research studies on the issues. We are exploring funding opportunities to undertake a study of Black women's health in the UK. Social disadvantage, social exclusion, racism and discrimination have all been linked to inequalities in health in Caribbean communities (Nazroo *et al.*, 2007). Despite the fact that some Caribbean people have lived in the UK for 50 or 60 years, these patterns of social disadvantage still persist. However, health-related issues are barely visible in Black feminist research in the UK, whereas in the US much Black feminist research focuses on health (Adams, 1995; Smith, 1995; Bayne-Smith, 1996; Roberts, 1999; Schulz and Mullings, 2006).

Conclusion

Black women academics need to have a vision and focus if they are to survive within higher education establishments, and to develop and maintain a supportive network. Health is an important focus for research yet it has often been ignored by Black feminist academics in the UK.

References

Adams, D.L. (ed.) (1995) *Health Issues for Women of Color: A cultural diversity perspective*. Thousand Oaks, CA: SAGE Publications.

Amos, V. and Parmar, P. (1984) 'Challenging imperial feminism'. *Feminist Review*, 17, 3–19.

Anthias, F. and Yuval-Davis, N. (1983) 'Contextualizing feminism: Gender, ethnic and class divisions'. *Feminist Review*, 15, 62–75.

Barn, R., Ladino, C. and Rogers, B. (2006) *Parenting in Multi-Racial Britain*. York: Joseph Rowntree Foundation.

Barriteau, V.E. (2006) 'The relevance of black feminist scholarship: A Caribbean perspective'. *Feminist Africa*, 7, 9–31.

Bayne-Smith, M. (ed.) (1996) *Race, Gender, and Health*. Thousand Oaks, CA: SAGE Publications.

Beishon, S., Virdee, S. and Hagell, A. (1995) *Nursing in a Multi-ethnic NHS*. London: Policy Studies Institute.

Bowleg, L. (2012) 'The problem with the phrase "women and minorities": Intersectionality – an important theoretical framework for public health'. *American Journal of Public Health*, 102 (7), 1267–73.

Boyce Davies, C. (2006) '"Con-di-fi-cation": Black women, leadership and political power'. *Feminist Africa*, 7, 67–88.

Brah, A. (1992) 'Difference, diversity and differentiation'. In Donald, J. and Rattansi, A. (eds) *'Race', Culture and Difference*. London: SAGE Publications, 126–45.

Brent Community Health Council (1981) *Black People and the Health Service*. London: Brent Community Health Council.

Bryan, B., Dadzie, S. and Scafe, S. (1985) *The Heart of the Race: Black women's lives in Britain*. London: Virago.

Burke, B., Cropper, A. and Harrison, P. (2000) 'Real or imagined: Black women's experiences in the academy'. *Community, Work and Family*, 3 (3), 297–310.

Carby, H.V. (1982) 'White woman listen! Black feminism and the boundaries of sisterhood'. In Centre for Contemporary Cultural Studies *The Empire Strikes Back: Race and racism in 70s Britain*. London: Hutchinson, 211–34.

Chamberlain, M. (2006) *Family Love in the Diaspora: Migration and the Anglo-Caribbean experience*. New Brunswick, NJ: Transaction Publishers.

Coard, B. (1971) *How the West Indian Child is Made Educationally Subnormal in the British School System: The scandal of the black child in schools in Britain*. London: New Beacon Books.

Cole, B.A. and Gunter, H. (eds) (2010) *Changing Lives: Women, inclusion and the PhD*. Stoke-on-Trent: Trentham Books.

Collingridge, D. and Douglas, J. (1984) 'Three models of policymaking: Expert advice in the control of environmental lead'. *Social Studies of Science*, 14 (3), 343–70.

Cottle, T.J. (1978) *Black Testimony: The voices of Britain's West Indians*. London: Wildwood House.

Crenshaw, K. (1989) 'Demarginalizing the intersection of race and sex: A black feminist critique of antidiscrimination doctrine, feminist theory and antiracist politics'. *University of Chicago Legal Forum*, 139–67.

Davidson, M.J. (1997) *The Black and Ethnic Minority Woman Manager: Cracking the concrete ceiling*. London: Paul Chapman Publishing.

Davis, A.Y. (1971) *If They Come in the Morning: Voices of resistance*. London: Orbach and Chambers.

— (1974) *Angela Davis: An autobiography*. NY: Random House.

— (1982) *Women, Race and Class*. London: Women's Press.

— (1990) *Women, Culture and Politics*. New York: Vintage Books.

— (1994) 'Sick and tired of being sick and tired: The politics of black women's health'. In White, E.C. (ed.) *The Black Women's Health Book: Speaking for ourselves*. Rev. ed. Seattle: Seal Press, 18–26.

Douglas, J. (1987) *Caribbean Food and Diet*. Cambridge: National Extension College for Training in Health and Race.

— (1991) 'I'm sick and tired of being sick and tired: A study of black women, health and health care'. Unpublished MA thesis, University of Warwick.

— (1995) 'Developing anti-racist health promotion strategies'. In Bunton, R., Nettleton, S. and Burrows, R. (eds) *The Sociology of Health Promotion: Critical analyses of consumption, lifestyle and risk*. London: Routledge, 70–7.

— (1996) 'Developing with black and minority ethnic communities, health promotion strategies which address social inequalities'. In Bywaters, P. and McLeod, E. (eds) *Working for Equality in Health*. London: Routledge, 179–96.

— (1997) 'Developing health promotion strategies with black and minority ethnic communities which address social inequalities'. In Sidell, M., Jones, L., Katz, J. and Peberdy, A. (eds) *Debates and Dilemmas in Promoting Health: A reader*. Basingstoke: Macmillan, 249–59.

— (2014) *African-Caribbean Young Women in the UK and Cigarette Smoking*. PhD thesis, University of York.

Douglas, J. and Watson, N. (2013) 'Resistance, resilience and renewal: The health and well-being of black women in the Atlantic diaspora: Developing an intersectional approach'. *Critical Public Health*, 23 (1), 1–5.

Fog Olwig, K. (2012) 'Migrating for an education: Family, gender and social mobility among Caribbean nurses in Britain'. Paper presented at San Diego University, November 2012.

Freire, P. (1972) *Pedagogy of the Oppressed*. Trans. Ramos, M.B. London: Penguin Books.

Goulbourne, H. (2002) *Caribbean Transnational Experience*. London: Pluto Press.

Green, A.L. and Scott, L.V. (eds) (2003) *Journey to the PhD: How to navigate the process as African Americans*. Sterling, VA: Stylus Publishing.

Gregory, S.T. (1999) *Black Women in the Academy: The secrets to success and achievement*. Rev. ed. Lanham, MD: University Press of America.

Gutiérrez y Muhs, G., Niemann, Y.F., González, C.G. and Harris, A.P. (eds) (2012) *Presumed Incompetent: The intersections of race and class for women in academia*. Boulder: University Press of Colorado.

hooks, b. (1982) *Ain't I a Woman: Black women and feminism*. London: Pluto Press.

James, W. (1993) 'Migration, racism and identity formation: The Caribbean experience in Britain'. In James, W. and Harris, C. (eds) *Inside Babylon: The Caribbean diaspora in Britain*. London: Verso, 231–88.

Jones, C. (2006) 'Falling between the cracks: What diversity means for black women in higher education'. *Policy Futures in Education*, 4 (2), 145–59.

Larbie, J. (1985) *Black Women and Maternity Services: A survey of 30 young Afro-Caribbean women's experiences and perceptions of pregnancy and childbirth*. London: Health Education Council and National Extension College for Training in Health and Race.

Levy, A. (2004) *Small Island*. London: Headline Review.

Liff, S. and Dale, K. (1994) 'Formal opportunity, informal barriers: Black women managers within a local authority'. *Work, Employment and Society*, 8 (2), 177–98.

Mekgwe, P. (2006) 'Theorizing African feminism(s): The "colonial" question'. *Quest: An African Journal of Philosophy*, 20 (1–2), 11–22.

Mirza, H.S. (1992) *Young, Female and Black*. London: Routledge.

— (1997) *Black British Feminism: A reader*. London: Routledge.

— (2006) 'Transcendence over diversity: Black women in the academy'. *Policy Futures in Education*, 4 (2), 101–13.

Mullings, L. (2000) 'African-American women making themselves: Notes on the role of Black feminist research'. *Souls: A Critical Journal of Black Politics, Culture, and Society,* 2 (4), 18–29.

Nazroo, J., Jackson, J., Karlsen, S. and Torres, M. (2007) 'The Black diaspora and health inequalities in the US and England: Does where you go and how you get there make a difference?'. *Sociology of Health and Illness*, 29 (6), 811–30.

Oyewumi, O. (ed.) (2003) *African Women and Feminism: Reflecting on the politics of sisterhood*. Trenton, NJ: Africa World Press.

Phoenix, A. (1988) 'Narrow definitions of culture: The case of early motherhood'. In Westwood, S. and Bhachu, P. (eds) *Enterprising Women: Ethnicity, economy, and gender relations*. London: Routledge, 121–39.

Reddock, R. (2007) 'Diversity, difference and Caribbean feminism: The challenge of anti-racism'. *Caribbean Review of Gender Studies*, 1, 1–24. Online. https:// sta.uwi.edu/crgs/april2007/journals/Diversity-Feb_2007.pdf (accessed 29 July 2017).

Reynolds, T. (2002) 'Re-thinking a black feminist standpoint'. *Ethnic and Racial Studies*, 25 (4), 591–606.

Roberts, D. (1999) *Killing the Black Body: Race, reproduction, and the meaning of liberty*. New York: Vintage Books.

Schulz, A.J. and Mullings, L. (eds) (2006) *Gender, Race, Class, and Health: Intersectional approaches*. San Francisco: Jossey-Bass.

Smith, S.L. (1995) *Sick and Tired of Being Sick and Tired: Black women's health activism in America, 1890–1950*. Philadelphia: University of Pennsylvania Press.

Stone, M. (1981) *The Education of the Black Child in Britain: The myth of multiracial education*. London: Fontana.

WHO (World Health Organization) (1985) *Targets for Health for All 2000*. Copenhagen: WHO Regional Office for Europe.

— (1986) *Ottawa Charter for Health Promotion*. Geneva: World Health Organization.

Wright, C., Thompson, S. and Channer, Y. (2007) 'Out of place: Black women academics in British universities'. *Women's History Review*, 16 (2), 145–62.

Young, L. (2000) 'What is black British feminism?'. *Women: A Cultural Review*, 11 (1–2), 45–60.

Chapter 8

The search for that elusive sense of belonging, respect and visibility in academia

Marcia Wilson

> *This chapter is dedicated to my parents: Leslie Samuel Wilson,*
> *3 July 1929 to 24 April 2017, and Fearn Merdena Wilson,*
> *10 July 1931 to 9 July 2017. On their shoulders I stand.*

Introduction

During my academic journey from the East End of London to America (via North Wales) and then back to the East End, I searched constantly for a feeling of belonging as a student and an academic. The sense of not being accepted and connected in academia made me feel I was invisible and didn't belong. However, this has been balanced by the positive experience of being at the forefront of institutional changes for students and staff. I have worked in academia for more than 25 years and, on a personal level, I would find it meaningful if this work results in other Black women having a different experience. Through my work, I strive to generate change so that under-represented groups can have a presence and a voice in academia.

My journey begins at the turn of the century. It was 2000 and I had finally completed my PhD. I remember feeling very accomplished as I walked across the stage during my graduation ceremony at the University of Iowa. After many years of hard work, I was finally a Doctor. I knew I would work as an academic and I vowed to make a positive difference to the many students I would encounter in the years to come. I was excited about the unknown possibilities and where my career would take me. I felt incredibly proud. I was the first person in my family to attend university and attain a PhD. I recognized this as a significant achievement because I am the daughter of Jamaican immigrants who lived then, and still live, in one of the poorest boroughs of the East End of London. I feel that successfully progressing through the education system can be extremely challenging for Black children, as their experience can be marred by low teacher expectations (Gershenson *et al.*, 2016) and hampered by institutional racism (Gillborn, 2005).

Following a telephone interview, I was offered a lecturing position at a university in the South West of England. I had spent one year after my graduation living and working at a small liberal arts college in South Carolina and the bubble had almost burst! Although the American college was a wonderful experience, I struggled with living in the Deep South. I found the traditional Southern hospitality in some areas but the racism was overwhelming in too many aspects of my life. When people found out that I was an academic at the local college I was respected, but when my identity was unknown I was treated quite differently. The racism experienced in South Carolina was extremely overt compared with the covert racism of the UK. I recall looking for somewhere to live when I first arrived in South Carolina and was gently guided to a neighbourhood where poor Whites and Black people lived. I continually heard racial slurs. Living in a place where overt racism was the norm was a step too far away from where I wanted my life to be as a professional Black woman. So I decided to see what the UK had to offer by way of an academic career.

On my first day in my new job in the UK, I toured the campus and met my colleagues in the Sport Science Department. Amid the lush green of the beautiful campus and welcoming smiles from my new colleagues, I felt exhilarated to be joining a community that was home to a range of famous institutions and international events. It is within this setting that I begin my reflective account of some key experiences that have shaped my academic career in England.

Invisible me

I was thrilled to be a lecturer in a university in the UK. I felt as though I had arrived! But within a very short time, it dawned on me that something was amiss. I had met everyone in my Sport Science Department and I was the only Black person working there. As I think about my early lecturing years, I am reminded of Roxanne Gay's reflective account of her first year as a professor and how this mirrors my experience:

> I am the child of immigrants. Many of my students have never had a Black teacher before. I can't help them with that. I'm the only Black professor in my department. This will probably never change for the whole of my career, no matter where I teach. I'm used to it. I wish I weren't. There seems to be some unspoken rule about the number of academic spaces people of color can occupy at the same time. I have grown weary of being the only one.
>
> (Gay, 2014: 22)

I carried on with my work but I never felt a sense of belonging in an environment of this kind. The department was overwhelmingly full of White men and it was not easy to break through the invisible barrier that separated me from the majority of my colleagues. I felt like one of Puwar's 'space invaders' (2004) in academia. I had earned the right to be there but never felt as though I actually belonged. Being in the extreme minority is not unusual for Black academics: academics of Black Caribbean ethnicity in permanent posts make up less than 1 per cent of UK academia (ECU, 2009). So it is hardly surprising that Black academics find themselves facing challenges that are much more extensive than the duties outlined in their job description (Cook, 1997). I found being in the minority very uncomfortable. I had a few allies, and felt supported by them, but I had to be vigilant regarding the students lest they perceived me to be an easy target for ridicule or racist jokes. I had experienced that before and wanted to quash such inappropriate behaviour from the beginning.

Since there were so few Black staff and students at the university, I was not surprised that there were few Black people in the town. The Black population was less than 1 per cent, compared with the national average of just over 3 per cent. The thing about living in a community where you are one of very few people of colour is that it impacts on almost everything you do. I was stared at every time I went out and followed by staff or security guards when I was shopping. My social life was constrained – every time I walked into a bar or restaurant, the room went slightly quieter as people noticed me. One of the most consistently frustrating experiences was trying to get served in bars or restaurants. I would simply be ignored – the staff acted as though they couldn't see me. I recall the feeling of continually being in a hostile environment, not belonging or feeling connected – and it was somewhere I could never call home. These experiences restricted my social life, because I felt that the places I could go to enjoy myself were limited. I also felt that my work was hampered by feeling unable to connect with the Whiteness of the institution.

For a long time, my invisibility permeated many areas of my academic life. I felt as though I was invisible in staff meetings and had to fight to get my voice heard. My contribution in such meetings was often overlooked or ignored and was definitely not acknowledged. I felt marginalized every time there was an event or meeting that required my presence. I was constantly reminded that I was an outsider by being ignored or having my contribution trivialized. Probably the worst irony was that being the only Black person in a largely White environment renders you anything but invisible. As Cook (1997) observes, the only time Black staff are truly visible is when they are absent! The experience of invisibility is so widespread that it can increase feelings of low self-worth and disrespect, a lack of justice, fragile sense of dignity and compromised personal identity (Franklin and Boyd-Franklin, 2000) – that is exactly how I felt. I was certain that if I stayed in this environment, the end result of continued invisibility would be psychological trauma (Franklin *et al.*, 2006).

I recall working at an open day where it was my role to promote the sport science programme we had on offer. I was standing by the table with the course leaflets available for prospective students, my name badge clearly displayed. When prospective students came to my table, they would ask me for Dr Marcia Wilson because they wanted to talk to her about sport science. Although I was wearing my staff ID card that clearly identified me as a university representative, there was a disconnect between my visual appearance as a Black female, and the role – as perceived by the visitors – of an academic member of staff who would be able to impart important information about the course. The disconnect was due to the culture and environment of UK universities. People's attitudes, thoughts and behaviour are shaped by their cultural beliefs. Cultural norms within universities are based on Eurocentric ideals. Therefore, there is an expectation that the academic staff will be White, whereas Black people are generally students. Traditionally, institutions are hierarchical as well as patriarchal (Nilsson and Nocon, 2005). There are few Black women within the hierarchy, and this is the case within sport science departments. They are patriarchal because academic scholars have generally been privileged White males (Henry, 1994).

Critical race theory (CRT) offers an appropriate and important framework to understand many of the experiences that I have encountered on my academic journey. One of the theoretical tenets of CRT is that race and racism are endemic, normalized and central to the functioning of our society (Delgado and Stefancic, 2001). I acknowledge that what happened at the open day could be seen as normal. Given the paucity of Black academics in the UK, it was 'normal' for prospective students and their parents to assume that I wasn't the person in charge. It was naturally assumed that my White colleagues were the academics and not me, notwithstanding my university ID. The many experiences of not being seen or regarded as an academic staff member, and how this misapprehension becomes normalized, induced in me feelings of marginalization. The overriding message was that I did not belong.

White male privilege

Peggy McIntosh (1988) is credited with popularizing the term 'White privilege' to describe assets that White people have and can cash in on a daily basis. McIntosh argues that White people, however, remain largely oblivious to these assets. She cites more than 50 privileges enjoyed by White people, such as their achievements not being regarded as exceptional, their mistakes not being attributed to biological inferiority, staff not following them around in shops and people not crossing the road to avoid them. Whiteness is seen as the norm or standard in Western society irrespective of social standing. White privilege is manifest in various arenas. For example, in the criminal justice system, Blacks are likely to receive harsher penalties than Whites for the same crime (Stevenson, 2014); in the education system, Black Caribbean children are three times more likely to be permanently excluded from school than their White counterparts (Bhattacharyya *et al.*, 2003); and in employment, individuals with a White-sounding name are more likely to be shortlisted for interview than those who have a name that indicates different ethnicity (Bertrand and Mullainathan, 2003). I witness such situations on a regular basis and try to raise awareness among my students about injustices of this kind.

The interlocking privileges associated with Whiteness and the male gender provide an important starting point for understanding many of the challenging experiences I've had within the academy. In the first year of my tenure in a new lecturing position at a more diverse university, an incident with a White student left me thinking about how White privilege plays out in the academy. I discovered that one of my final-year students had plagiarized a significant part of his dissertation. And he had not engaged with the supervisory process. Following an investigation, the student was required to retake the whole of the final year (it emerged that there were issues in some of his other modules too). However, following an appeal and a misconduct meeting, the student was invited simply to rewrite his dissertation. It transpired that he had informed the university that he had plagiarized because he had received poor academic supervision – whereas he had never once attended a tutorial.

I was left wondering whether this would have been the outcome if the lecturer had been a White middle-class man, or if the student had been Black. I also questioned whether the student and his father would have verbally attacked a White male in the same way and whether the university officials would have told the student in my presence that he would be assigned a more experienced supervisor. No one can say for certain, but I do believe that my colleagues and the student found it easier to demonize a new Black female member of staff. Black women in academia are a rarity, often regarded as the 'other', which makes us an easier target to attack. Every person in the academic misconduct meeting about the plagiarizer was a White male – except me. The corridor that led to the meeting room was adorned with large portraits of White men who have held positions of power in the university. The surrounding imagery informed everyone who took notice that this was a place where White men belonged and if you did not fit that mould, you were the 'other'. Being physically present in that room and in that situation, it was extremely clear to me that White cultural values were dominant and that they permeated the university.

Examining that experience from a critical perspective, it is clear that my race, gender and class interlocked (Collins, 1990) and were the binary opposite to the norm in the institution: historically the preserve of the White, middle-class male, who represents academic competence. The opposite (Black, working-class woman) represents incompetence (Anthony, 2012). This episode added to my feelings of marginalization and lack of support. Wright and colleagues (2007) note that experiences of this kind are common among Black female academics in the UK. My overriding feeling was that I had been caught up in an old boys' network and had done something terribly wrong. I felt as though any academic credibility gained during my short career had been wiped out in one fell swoop.

As I thought about what the powers that be at the university saw when they looked at me, my father's words echoed loudly in my ears, 'Cut your hair. If you want to get on, they need to see you differently. You'll have to cut your hair.' I wear dreadlocks, which are long, thick and permanent. I choose to wear my hair in this style because I wish to embrace my cultural heritage and identity. Many of my students identify with my style and I frequently receive compliments about it on campus. But I recognize that my hair is not the norm for academic staff and this has contributed to the disrespect I have encountered. Throughout this whole episode, the politics of respectability ran through my mind. Gay (2014) asserts that thinking this way is aligned with behaving in a culturally approved manner and that individuals strive thus to gain acceptance from the dominant culture. However, as Gay rightly argues, the politics of respectability does not take into account many of the issues raised earlier about the racial discrimination permeating the justice system, educational institutions and employability practices.

Although the demographic of students in certain universities has changed considerably over recent years, it is important to remember that certain students still struggle with the imposter syndrome (Jarrett, 2010) and feel as though they don't belong in higher education. I have been through this and know how vital it is to maintain my core beliefs and remember my working-class roots. Anthony (2012) makes a good point about staying true to yourself: 'If you turn your back on it for career success, you pass up a chance to change the world, and the "you" that succeeds is not your authentic self.' After this incident, I was more determined than ever to succeed in academia but it was important for me to be myself and not conform to society's view of what an academic looks like.

I immersed myself in my work as a lecturer in sport science. I strove to hone my craft in teaching and make the sessions as creative and inclusive as possible. I made it my business to know and support my students. I loved their company and that they came to see me quite often in my office to talk about their lives. I am thankful for every student with whom I have been privileged to share their academic journey. A few years ago, my students nominated me for a teaching award. More than 400 lecturers across the institution were nominated. When the vice chancellor read out my name as the winner, I felt honoured, uplifted and knew that my hard work was recognized by those who mattered the most – my students. The award helped me come to terms with some of the unpleasant experiences earlier in my career, especially the times when my competence was openly questioned by senior management. Knowing that my students appreciated my efforts helped me to stay in academia and motivated me to continue my work.

Where are all the Black leaders in higher education?

I had previously applied for low-level leadership positions but was not successful. On one occasion a colleague had been invited to take on the role on an interim basis, and on another the department head consulted selected members of the team to ask who they thought should be the successful individual and, after meeting with the person they nominated, he was appointed to the leadership role.

Although I have always enjoyed teaching and the company of my students, I was feeling incredibly frustrated over the many experiences of invisibility and patriarchy. I needed greater control and more of a voice so I could effectively challenge and fight what I witnessed and experienced on a regular basis in the academy. When I reflect on my career during the early stages, I don't remember consciously telling myself that I wanted to be a manager or a leader, but the thought must have been lurking somewhere in my sub-conscious. Although career progression is slower for women than men in general (Quinn, 2012), it seems that career progression for Black women in academia is not only slow but also extremely limited. This is reflected in the highest positions of power in universities across the UK: there are no Black female vice chancellors or deputy vice chancellors. The recent appointment in 2015 of Baroness Amos as the Director of the School of Oriental and African Studies (SOAS, 2015) is a step in the right direction.

The picture is dismal further down the management chain where, out of 3,220 heads of major academic departments and heads of schools, only 20 are Black (Rathi and Ware, 2014). There are more than 19,600 professors in the UK; 110 are Black and only 30 are Black women (Black British Academics, 2016). These figures are shocking and clearly indicate that Black people are severely under-represented in the higher echelons of academia, especially Black women. However, knowing that the situation is so bad and there are so many barriers ahead strengthens my resolve to progress in higher education. It took a while but I made a conscious decision to work towards becoming a manager and leader. I needed to have a voice to fight the many injustices I regularly experienced and witnessed.

When an opportunity arose to lead the undergraduate sport programmes, I quickly expressed interest and was appointed to the role. I was finally on my way to generating some change in my institution. As the sport programmes became more successful, structural changes within my school resulted in the creation of a Sport Science Department. I interviewed for the department head position and accepted the offer of the permanent job. My current role is Associate Dean in one of the largest schools within my university and I am immensely proud to have this position. When it was announced that I had been appointed, I was taken aback by the outpouring of genuine delight and respect expressed by colleagues within the university and across the sector. However, I also think that many of the good wishes came from people who were just pleased, and to a certain extent relieved, to see a Black woman in a management role. I have worked in a management role for around six years and continually strive to fulfil my promise that my students would benefit from my actions. My students have been wonderfully supportive. If the truth be known, I see myself in many of them. The majority are from Black and minority ethnic backgrounds; many are first-generation university students from working-class families in the East End of London. I see their struggles as racialized minorities who are trying their utmost to succeed in their chosen field.

One valuable lesson about promotion that I learnt along the way is that it is important to have a plan of action if you express an interest in a position, especially if Black women are under-represented in the job you wish to move to. At one of the universities where I worked, a vacancy at a higher level arose. When I declared my interest to a rather shocked White manager, he made it perfectly clear that he had not considered me a suitable fit for the role. I approached him three times to find out why he felt that way. I was never given a satisfactory answer and, in the final meeting, I was informed that the appointment would be for an external rather than an internal candidate. I felt saddened that I had been working in academia for more than ten years and was still having to fight the blatant discrimination that so regularly surfaced. And I was angry because I had done everything I was supposed to do – I had engaged in high-quality teaching (student evaluations testify to this), published papers and secured funding for research. I was at a loss as to what more I needed to do to advance in my career. This experience is not unlike that of other Black female academics. Showunmi and Maylor (2013) recount what happened when one of them applied for promotion and it did not materialize due to lack of management support, although she carried a workload concomitant with the requirements of the higher grade.

I was disappointed but not beaten. I reframed the experience in a positive manner: the exchange with the manager enabled me to see what he thought about me. I told myself that I was lucky to have had that initial conversation because now I knew what the challenges were. I took on higher-level projects in addition to my duties and worked at least 65 hours a week to ensure that the interview panel had no reason to reject me if I was shortlisted. I applied for the job as soon as it was advertised and was offered the position. Although I was elated, I felt a twinge of disappointment that it had required such effort to get the job.

Early in my management career, I encountered many challenges, although I must stress that most colleagues were supportive. But a few were disrespectful, repeatedly challenging my authority. Most common is their lack of eye contact when in conversation with me, or their failure to reply to emails and messages, or to acknowledge me on campus. Black women who hold management positions find such behaviour is commonplace (Holder *et al.*, 2015; Maürtin-Cairncross, 2009). This 'othering' process is a way of letting Black women know that, whatever their position of power in the academy, they still don't belong. In time, I developed the confidence to challenge any disrespectful behaviour and developed effective strategies for addressing it, such as respectfully pointing out any discrimination immediately. Whether or not the disrespectful behaviour is aimed at me, I challenge the person who has transgressed. I have zero tolerance for discrimination or injustice. I am aware that some colleagues find a Black feminist manager disconcerting and I make no apology for that, but I do recognize that is where the backlash has come from. Colleagues are not used to hearing a Black woman voice issues that are problematic. However, it is the same colleagues who fail to acknowledge that racism and sexism are prevalent throughout the university structures who want to maintain the status quo so their privilege remains intact. They see no need for change.

Educational injustice

As a Black female manager working in an institution where about 66 per cent of the students identify as Black or minority ethnic, I am in a strong position to draw attention to issues of educational injustice. One of the key areas is the attainment gap between students of different ethnicities across the sector (Berry and Loke, 2011). This gap is the difference between a 'good' degree – a 1st or a 2:1 – and a 2:2 or 3rd. Over the past ten years, the gap has remained relatively static with 73.2 per cent of White British students attaining a 'good' degree compared with 57.1 per cent of Black and minority ethnic students. However, there are stark attainment differences within the Black and minority ethnic groups. For example, the following attain a 'good' degree: 64.4 per cent of Indian students, 63.9 per cent of Chinese students, 54.2 per cent of Pakistani students and only 43.8 per cent of Black Other students (Berry and Loke, 2011).

The exact cause of the attainment gap is unknown. However, what is clear is that there are multiple, intersecting factors that might have an effect, such as unconscious and implicit bias (Banaji and Greenwald, 2016), stereotype threat (Steele and Aronson, 1995; Steele, 2010) and the lack of expectation held by staff for students (Brophy, 1983; Wilson and Stephens, 2007). Over the years I have tried hard to get across how important it is for academics to hold high expectations of students, whatever their background. I am very aware of this from my PhD research where I examined the expectations held by coaches of high-school basketball players. Although my research was in the domain of sport, the outcomes apply equally to the education context (Rosenthal and Jacobson, 1968).

I seek to highlight to White colleagues how important it is that they hold high expectations for Black students. The research has consistently demonstrated that Black teachers have higher expectations for Black students than White teachers do (Beady and Hansell, 1981; Gershenson *et al.*, 2016). In fact, this has been openly discussed when working with some White colleagues. A White male academic remarked to me that when he sees young Asian men sitting at the back of the lecture theatre, he feels that they are not engaged in the class and does not expect academic excellence from them. Unfortunately, when low expectations are communicated to students, even unwittingly, the students expect less of themselves. This perpetuates the tiered society, adhering to the unequal structures that White people seldom see.

Allowing every student the opportunity to give their best is crucial if we are going to make a difference. We know that more Black students withdraw from their degree programme than any other group (HEFCE, 2011), so encouraging them to complete their degree is vital, but the importance of attaining a 'good' degree should not be underestimated. Many universities require students to have a minimum of a 2:1 if they wish to apply for a postgraduate qualification and so do jobs at graduate level. It follows that, if this trend continues, there will be a lack of diversity in graduate-level jobs across the sector. A recent report revealed that Black graduates face greater difficulty than their White counterparts in securing employment after graduation (55.4 per cent of Black Caribbean graduates enter professional employment after graduation compared with 64.7 per cent of White British). Furthermore, when they do secure graduate-level positions, they earn 23 per cent less than White graduates (TUC, 2016). These statistics flag the need for universities across the sector to examine and amend their practice.

As the Race Equality Charter Mark lead for my university, I am involved in many projects being piloted to raise awareness and bring about positive change for our students and staff. I have worked tirelessly with colleagues to enable all staff to start having conversations about race and racism in the academy. I have supported projects such as the Many Voices Reading Group developed by Dr Julie Botticello in the School of Health, Sport and Bioscience at the University of East London. The group meets once a fortnight to critically discuss that session's recommended readings: short chapters or articles by Black authors from across the globe that seldom feature in the mainstream curriculum. The themes range from Black feminism (Adichie, 2014), to female genital mutilation (Wardere, 2016), to incarceration and capital punishment (Davis, 2003; Williams, 2006) and activism (Saro-Wiwa, 1995). The wonderful thing about this group is that, although attendance is voluntary, students opt to attend in droves, reading the selected pieces beforehand. They tell me how this project facilitates their learning of the core curriculum because they gain knowledge about key concepts they can identify with and this then builds on what they are learning in lectures. The students are enthused by their reading and carry on discussing social justice issues long after the sessions finish.

A couple of years ago, I tried to engage the mostly White male sport science staff in the concept of feminism. I asked colleagues to read *We Should All Be Feminists* by Adichie (2014), in an attempt to highlight the situation of the female students in the department, who are in the minority and feel marginalized on the sport science programme. Also, more importantly, I felt that as leaders of the courses we are in a powerful position and we should have feminism at the forefront of our consciousness when designing and delivering sport modules for all. I tried to emphasize that we should think about the content of the curriculum through the eyes of our students. If we do not consider women in sport, the content and delivery of the curriculum will remain too male-dominated. My request that they read Adichie's short essay was met with a mixture of resistance and willingness to understand. I think that starting the (often difficult) conversations about gender, race, class, homophobia, etc. is the most important first step to generating change.

With regards to closing the gaps in attainment, I have tried to shift the focus away from a student deficit model and towards implementing changes in the curriculum and its delivery so that it becomes more inclusive. If we are to achieve equality in education, the current system clearly needs transformation. The curriculum needs to move away from perpetuating elite White male scholarship as the norm and instead represent a range of key sources of knowledge (Collins, 1991).

Conclusion

Reflecting on my journey in academia, I can see that it would have made a positive difference to me as a student if I had been able to read and discuss a wide range of literature by many diverse authors. The literature assigned for my undergraduate and master's curricula was largely authored by White men. It was only when I was doing my PhD that the curriculum and the resources were more diverse. Through most of my academic career as a student, I felt deprived of learning about any topics that were not White and male. It was up to me alone to look beyond what was set as the academic norm to discover a whole new world of diverse scholarship. I valued this scholarship but this knowledge was not regarded by the powers that be as of significant worth.

I would also have valued having more Black women as lecturers and seeing Black academics in senior management positions. Throughout my three degrees, I was only taught by one Black woman professor: Dr Audrey Qualls. She was a phenomenal person, a mentor and role model to me during my PhD. She inspired me to be the best I could possibly be and to stay strong while weathering the racial storms in the academy.

There are issues within the education system that require urgent attention. That Black staff feel marginalized and unsupported, have their ability questioned and experience difficulties in gaining promotion have been well documented (e.g. Bhopal *et al.*, 2016). Real change is needed in universities where Black staff and students can feel a sense of belonging and are valued for their contributions. Audre Lorde encapsulates this exact point when, almost 40 years ago at the Second Sex Conference in New York in 1979, she declared:

> Those of us who stand outside the circle of this society's definition of acceptable women; those of us who have been forged in the crucible of difference – those of us who are poor, who are lesbians, who are Black, who are older – know that survival is not an academic skill. It is learning how to stand alone, unpopular and sometimes reviled … It is learning how to take our differences and make them strengths. For the master's tools will never dismantle the master's house. They may enable us temporarily to beat him at his own game, but they will never enable us to bring about genuine change.
>
> (Lorde, 1984: 112)

To bring about real change, the racial make-up of the senior echelons of universities will need to become far more diverse. Much work needs to done before all students are enabled to achieve their full potential and the existing gaps in attainment, employment and earnings are closed. These objectives will be achieved when the decision-makers in organizations commit to delivering fairness, equality and social justice and put them at the forefront of their agenda. Some years ago, I made a decision that I would devote my time and effort to furthering racial equality. We will live in a better, fairer world when the barriers to success are permanently torn down.

References
Adichie, C.N. (2014) *We Should All Be Feminists*. New York: Vintage Books.

Anthony, C.G. (2012) 'The Port Hueneme of my mind: The geography of working-class consciousness in one academic career'. In Gutiérrez y Muhs, G., Niemann, Y.F., González, C.G. and Harris, A.P. (eds) *Presumed Incompetent: The intersections of race and class for women in academia*. Boulder: University Press of Colorado, 300–12.

Banaji, M.R. and Greenwald, A.G. (2016) *Blindspot: Hidden biases of good people*. London: Penguin Random House.

Beady, C.H. and Hansell, S. (1981) 'Teacher race and expectations for student achievement'. *American Educational Research Journal*, 18 (2), 191–206.

Berry, J. and Loke, G. (2011) *Improving the Degree Attainment of Black and Minority Ethnic Students*. London: Equality Challenge Unit / HEA.

Bertrand, M. and Mullainathan, S. (2003) *Are Emily and Greg More Employable than Lakisha and Jamal? A field experiment on labor market discrimination* (Working Paper 9873). Cambridge, MA: National Bureau of Economic Research.

Bhattacharyya, G., Ison, L. and Blair, M. (2003) *Minority Ethnic Attainment and Participation in Education and Training: The evidence* (Research Topic Paper RTP01-03). Nottingham: Department for Education and Skills.

Bhopal, K., Brown, H. and Jackson, J. (2016) 'BME academic flight from UK to overseas higher education: Aspects of marginalisation and exclusion'. *British Educational Research Journal*, 42 (2), 240–57.

Black British Academics (2016) 'HESA statistics professors by race and gender'. Online. http://blackbritishacademics.co.uk/focus/hesa-statistics-professors-by-race-and-gender (accessed 29 July 2017).

Brophy, J.E. (1983) 'Research on the self-fulfilling prophecy and teacher expectations'. *Journal of Educational Psychology*, 75 (5), 631–61.

Collins, P.H. (1990) *Black Feminist Thought: Knowledge, consciousness, and the politics of empowerment.* London: Routledge.

— (1991) 'On our own terms: Self-defined standpoints and curriculum transformation'. *NWSA Journal*, 3 (3), 367–81.

Cook, D. (1997) 'The art of survival in white academia: Black women faculty finding where they belong'. In Fine, M., Weis, L., Powell, L.C. and Wong, L.M. (eds) *Off White: Readings on race, power, and society.* New York: Routledge, 100–9.

Davis, A.Y. (2003) *Are Prisons Obsolete?* New York: Seven Stories Press.

Delgado, R. and Stefancic, J. (2001) *Critical Race Theory: An introduction.* New York: New York University Press.

ECU (Equality Challenge Unit) (2009) *The Experience of Black and Minority Ethnic Staff Working in Higher Education in England.* Online. http://www.ecu. ac.uk/wp-content/uploads/external/experience-of-bme-staff-in-he-final-report. pdf (accessed 12 September 2017).

Franklin, A.J. and Boyd-Franklin, N. (2000) 'Invisibility syndrome: A clinical model of the effects of racism on African-American males'. *American Journal of Orthopsychiatry,* 70 (1), 33–41.

Franklin, A.J., Boyd-Franklin, N. and Kelly, S. (2006) 'Racism and invisibility: Race-related stress, emotional abuse and psychological trauma for people of color'. *Journal of Emotional Abuse*, 6 (2–3), 9–30.

Gay, R. (2014) *Bad Feminist: Essays.* London: Corsair.

Gershenson, S., Holt, S.B. and Papageorge, N.W. (2016) 'Who believes in me? The effect of student–teacher demographic match on teacher expectations'. *Economics of Education Review*, 52, 209–24.

Gillborn, D. (2005) 'Education policy as an act of white supremacy: Whiteness, critical race theory and education reform'. *Journal of Education Policy*, 20 (4), 485–505.

HEFCE (Higher Education Funding Council for England) (2011) *Non-continuation rates: trends and profiles.* Online. http://www.hefce.ac.uk/analysis/ncr/nc (accessed 12 September 2017).

Henry, M. (1994) 'Ivory towers and ebony women: The experiences of Black women in higher education'. In Davies, S., Lubelska, C. and Quinn, J. (eds) *Changing the Subject: Women in higher education*. London: Taylor and Francis, 42–57.

Holder, A.M.B., Jackson, M.A. and Ponterotto, J.G. (2015) 'Racial microaggression experiences and coping strategies of Black women in corporate leadership'. *Qualitative Psychology*, 2 (2), 164–80.

Jarrett, C. (2010) 'Feeling like a fraud'. *The Psychologist*, 23 (5), 380–3.

Lorde, A. (1984) *Sister Outsider: Essays and speeches*. Freedom, CA: Crossing Press.

Maürtin-Cairncross, A. (2009) 'A still-chilly climate: Experiences of women in leadership positions in South African higher education'. *On Campus with Women*, 38 (1). Online. http://archive.aacu.org/ocww/volume38_1/global.cfm (accessed 29 July 2017).

McIntosh, P. (1988) *White Privilege and Male Privilege: A personal account of coming to see correspondences through work in women's studies*. Online. www. collegeart.org/pdf/diversity/white-privilege-and-male-privilege.pdf (accessed 29 July 2017).

Nilsson, M. and Nocon, H. (2005) 'Practicing invisibility: Women's roles in higher education'. *Outlines: Critical Practice Studies*, 7 (1), 14–30.

Puwar, N. (2004) 'Fish in or out of water: A theoretical framework for race and the space of academia'. In Law, I., Phillips, D. and Turney, L. (eds) *Institutional Racism in Higher Education*. Stoke-on-Trent: Trentham Books, 49–58.

Quinn, J. (2012) *Mentoring: Progressing women's careers in higher education*. London: Equality Challenge Unit. Online. www.ecu.ac.uk/wp-content/uploads/external/mentoring-progressing-womens-careers-in-higher-education.pdf (accessed 29 July 2017).

Rathi, A. and Ware, G. (2014) 'Race and academia: Diversity among UK university students and leaders'. *The Conversation*, 9 April. Online. http://theconversation.com/race-and-academia-diversity-among-uk-university-students-and-leaders-24988 (accessed 29 July 2017).

Rosenthal, R. and Jacobson, L. (1968) *Pygmalion in the Classroom: Teacher expectation and pupils' intellectual development*. New York: Holt, Rinehart and Winston.

Saro-Wiwa, K. (1995) *A Month and a Day: A detention diary*. London: Penguin.

Showunmi, V. and Maylor, U. (2013) 'Black women reflecting on being Black in the academy'. MS. UCL Institute of Education.

SOAS (School of Oriental and African Studies) (2015) 'Valerie Amos to be ninth director of SOAS, University of London'. SOAS press release, 29 June. Online. www.soas.ac.uk/news/newsitem103350.html (accessed 10 March 2017).

Steele, C.M. (2010) *Whistling Vivaldi: How stereotypes affect us and what we can do*. New York: W.W. Norton and Company.

Steele, C.M. and Aronson, J. (1995) 'Stereotype threat and the intellectual test performance of African Americans'. *Journal of Personality and Social Psychology*, 69 (5), 797–811.

Stevenson, B. (2014) *Just Mercy: A story of justice and redemption*. New York: Spiegel and Grau.

TUC (Trades Union Congress) (2016) 'Black workers with degrees earn a quarter less than white counterparts, finds TUC'. TUC press release, 1 February. Online. www.tuc.org.uk/equality-issues/black-workers/labour-market/black-workers-degrees-earn-quarter-less-white (accessed 29 July 2017).

Wardere, H. (2016) *Cut: One woman's fight against FGM in Britain today*. London: Simon and Schuster.

Williams, S.T. (2006) *Redemption: From original gangster to Nobel Prize nominee*. London: Maverick House.

Wilson, M.A. and Stephens, D.E. (2007) 'Great expectations: An examination of the differences between high and low expectancy athletes' perception of coach treatment'. *Journal of Sport Behavior*, 30 (3), 358–73.

Wright, C., Thompson, S. and Channer, Y. (2007) 'Out of place: Black women academics in British universities'. *Women's History Review*, 16 (2), 145–62.

Chapter 9

The transformation of my science identity

Elizabeth Opara

Introduction

My love of science led me to a world I believed I belonged in – until I experienced an event that shook my faith in the science academy, and brought back to me the words of my parents: 'you will always have to be ten times as good'. Articulating this experience, its impact on my identity as a scientist, and the subsequent transformation of this identity, has been a difficult endeavour but a necessary one that has allowed me to find my voice as a Black woman scientist.

Articulating my journey

I am a scientist through and through. I have been trained to write in a way that is detached and does not reveal who I am. So when I was asked to contribute to this body of work, I knew it would be a struggle to articulate my experiences as a scientist who is both Black and a woman, in the context of Black feminism. To assist me, I turned to material that focused on women scientists in the academy and one study stood out – the research carried out by Carlone and Johnson (2007) on understanding better how science identities are developed, in the context of race and gender. This study resonated with me from its first critical question: how do women of colour exist and persist in an environment 'characterized by White, masculine values and behavioural norms, hidden within an ideology of meritocracy'? (1,187). Literature on the success of women of colour in science identifies pre-college science experiences, family support, intrinsic motivation and perseverance as being critical to this success (Russell and Atwater, 2005) and these factors have all played a major role in my persistence in the science environment. However, Carlone and Johnson (2007) point out that such literature does not explicitly address how race, ethnicity and gender impact, influence and complicate these factors. They argue that the construct of identity could potentially explain this interplay and thus developed a model of science identity. The model, informed by the literature, contains three overlapping dimensions: competence (knowledge and understanding of science), performance (ability to communicate science in a variety of settings and proficiency in the laboratory) and recognition (by oneself and others as being a 'science person'). The model was used to analyse and thus make sense of the experiences of a group of successful women of colour within the science environment. The model reveals the recognition dimension 'made most visible the interactions between the women's science identity trajectories and their race, ethnicity and gender' (1,197). It is the authors' focus on the impact of recognition of one's science identity that enables me to make sense of, and articulate the impact of, an experience that has profoundly affected my identity and thus my journey as a Black woman scientist.

My science identity: From recognition to disruption

For as long as I can remember I have loved science in all its simplicity and its complexity, although I have always been aware that my race and gender have affected the way in which I am perceived by others – culturally, politically, sexually and socially. As a scientist and academic, I never saw myself as being different from the norm. I believed I belonged because we, my fellow scientists and I, all had one thing in common – a love of science – a love that I believed made us equal. I enjoyed science subjects at school, especially chemistry. As an undergraduate, I embraced the study of biochemistry with a fervour that had me buried in the laboratory with my research project in my final year. I pursued my love of scientific research by completing my PhD in nutritional biochemistry, a study of glutamine metabolism in skeletal muscle, adipose tissue (fat) and cells of the immune system. I looked at glutamine, an amino acid that research suggests plays an important role in maintaining immune function in conditions of stress, for example injury. My interest in the subject of my PhD research stemmed from a desire to extend my knowledge and understanding of biochemistry in a clinical context. Following my PhD, I continued with post-doctoral work in both the US and the UK, broadening my portfolio of laboratory competence and honing my research skills while I also developed interests in other areas of nutritional biochemistry, specifically the bioactive properties of food. I then successfully applied for my first academic post as a lecturer.

The passage to my first academic post is acknowledged as the traditional route in science: undergraduate degree to PhD to post-doctoral to lecturer, and so to me it meant that I belonged. It is the same sense of belonging felt by the women in the study by Carlone and Johnson (2007) at the beginning of their journey as scientists. However, what resonates most with me in this study is their research science identity, an identity that had me nodding in animated recognition. The women in the study 'saw science as an exciting way of knowing, expressed the importance of science for science's sake, and conveyed an interest in studying the natural world' (1,197). They engaged enthusiastically with research as undergraduates and 'began to *imagine* themselves fitting into their community of practice' (1,198) and, by pursuing research as undergraduates, provided themselves with ways 'of *aligning* their actions and energies with others further along the research scientist trajectory' (1,198). This articulation of the research identity spoke volumes to me, as I too imagined my place in the science community when I was an undergraduate and by pursuing postgraduate and post-doctoral research I followed the traditional path taken by so many others.

My belief that I belonged was reinforced by the recognition I received from established members of the scientific community – all White and male – as was the case for the women of colour in Carlone and Johnson's study (2007). In my case, this recognition came through co-authoring papers, presenting at national and international conferences, and beginning to peer-review papers. Furthermore, these activities reinforced my own self-recognition as a research scientist who had also been given the opportunity to share her love, knowledge and understanding of science with her students. At this time, early in my career, I did not have to struggle to gain acceptance in my field – a story that is not uncommon (Hirshfield and Joseph, 2012). Consequently, not only did I believe I belonged, I also naïvely believed that the science academy was a level playing field.

At this point in my science journey I never considered that my race and gender had impacted, or would impact, on my research science identity. In hindsight, this is surprising in light of the paucity of Black women in science. In its report on improving diversity in science, technology, engineering and maths (STEM), the Campaign for Science and Engineering (CaSE, 2014: 42) reported that, of the women studying STEM subjects in higher education during 2009/10, 8 per cent were Black Caribbean and 25 per cent were Black African, yet very few Black women pursue research-based higher degrees. Such a disparity stems from society's association of Blackness with sports and entertainment, not with science and intellect, thus sending a message that Black women have no place in science. However, some argue that my reasons for recognizing myself as a research scientist could be ascribed to anyone who is pursuing a career as a research scientist, regardless of their race and gender. Such an argument can only be made if one assumes that I was able to keep to this trajectory – underpinned as it was by my self-recognition as a research scientist, which was greatly influenced by the recognition of established others.

The disruption of my research science identity

Once appointed to my first academic post, I progressed from lecturer to senior lecturer within two years, picking up a course leadership along the way. Two years later, I had a PhD student and was continuing to build my research portfolio through conference presentations, science publications and peer reviewing. Then in late 2004, a promotion opportunity arose in field leadership, which came with a principal lectureship. Two people went for the post – me (the internal applicant) and an applicant from another institution. They offered the post to my competitor – a White man. I was told that it was a close call, but that was little consolation – and was the extent of the feedback I received. I expected detailed feedback as to why I was unsuccessful, but instead I was left to speculate about the reasons for their decision not to promote me. The emotions this decision aroused were disappointment and frustration, the latter because I was effectively already doing the job and doing it well. These emotions gave way to anger and also confusion. I had interviewed well, or so I thought, and the academy is all about meritocracy (is it not?). There were only two obvious reasons left as to why I was not offered the job and why I received virtually no feedback: my race and my gender. In subsequent discussions with family and close friends, the words that I had heard as a 5-year-old came up time and time again: 'you have to be ten times better'. In 2004, I still had to be ten times better!

The literature tells us much about how the academy, despite its belief that it is neutral, objective and open-minded, is actually none of these things. The academy embodies the society within which it exists and so the gender and racial inequities that exist in our society exist within the academy (Hiraldo, 2010; Jones, 2006; Mirza, 2006; Ramohai, 2014; Wright *et al.*, 2007). In their paper on buffering the impact of the science workplace's negative climate on women scientists, Settles and others (2007: 270–1) talk of perceptions such as mine not needing to be 'accurate assessments of the organization (Seibert *et al.*, 2004), nor must they agree with others' perceptions in the same environment to be meaningful and consequential, because each individual's environment may be distinctive (Rousseau, 1998)'. I accept this point of view but my perceptions of this experience are strongly validated when explained in the context of Carlone and Johnson's (2007) findings according to their science identity model. My experience gave rise to what they called a disruption of my science identity brought about by established others within science who, at the time of the interview, recognized me not as a scientist but as a representative of a stigmatized group (Carlone and Johnson, 2007). I believe their focus on my race and gender stopped them from seeing me as a scientist and as a science leader.

Ultimately, this experience affected my recognition of self as a scientist and left me contemplating leaving science altogether. I believed that being Black and female was at the heart of their decision but I had never asked myself what being Black and a woman and a scientist meant to them. Together these meant that I did not belong. My gender did not conform to norms that are 'aligned with masculine practices' and behaviours that pervade the science world (Carlone and Johnson, 2007: 1,204) and are 'consistent with gender-normative prescriptions of men (e.g., objective, rational, single minded)' (Settles *et al.*, 2007: 271) and the culture of science being 'aggressive and competitive' (ibid.). What is professionally essential then is looking, talking, acting, thinking and interacting in ways that conform to notions of what and how a scientist should be and behave that are steeped in the history and culture of the White hegemonic society (Carlone and Johnson, 2007). Such behaviours and environments permit fewer opportunities for women, particularly in leadership roles. Job satisfaction is diminished, attrition and stagnation are the result (CaSE, 2014: 43; Hill *et al.*, 2010: 68; Settles *et al.*, 2007: 271).

On the issue of race, Carlone and Johnson (2007) talk of racially disrupted recognition, which they identify in their study, and draw on the literature (Lewis, 2006; Parsons and Mutegi, 2007) to emphasize the importance of being aware of the ways in which race can negatively influence the decisions made by established others. Most of the Black women in their study reported experiences where their recognition as scientists, by scientists, was disrupted, suggesting that nuanced racism was at play. Racism of this kind is now openly acknowledged and discussed (Bhopal, 2016; Else, 2014, 2015; Grove, 2013, 2015, 2016; Hunt, 2016; Morgan, 2016; Reisz, 2015; Rollock, 2016; Williams, 2013).

Surviving with my disrupted science identity

I was eventually offered the job I had gone for at my university – by default, after the rival candidate used the offer as leverage for a promotion at his own institution. I accepted the job but the whole ordeal subdued me. I stagnated for fear of further rejection. I was just going through the motions of teaching and doing research without making concrete career decisions – but I stayed. Why? Carlone and Johnson (2007) asked the very same question of the women of colour, whose science identity was disrupted but who are still pursuing science-related careers. What they learnt from this group is that discrimination is not destiny (1,209). Although I believe this to be true – because we women of colour who are scientists and in the science environment are living proof of it – it did not fully answer my question.

However, when Carlone and Johnson (2007) went on to ask whether the women's persistence was due to 'their commitment to science' and/or 'the presence of others' support or recognition' and/or 'positive experiences with science outside the university' (1,209), I found my answer. I remained because of my commitment to science and because I had recognition and support from others. Teaching and research bolstered me, combined with words of wisdom from those closest to me – 'do not give up', 'you are more than good at what you do' and 'remember you are Ada'. Ada is short for Adannaya ('her father's daughter') and is used in my family's Igbo culture to recognize the importance of the first-born daughter. For me, and for all first-born Igbo daughters, it is a tool of empowerment because we are brought up to believe that we can achieve all that we set our minds to; we can deal with any challenge (Odoaje, 2014). These words allowed me to survive, despite being initially turned down for the promotion and the consequent disruption of my science identity. Even so, the fear of further humiliation never went away and I became frustrated with myself – for stagnating out of fear – and with the science environment – which was oblivious to my disrupted science identity. In their excellent report on the price of being a woman of colour in science, Malcom and colleagues (1976) articulate clearly, from the experiences of women of colour, the high emotional, personal and professional costs these women incurred in following science careers. Obviously I too was paying the same high price for staying in science, but I remained in my disrupted science identity for six years. Then, a conversation born out of my frustration sparked a change that resulted in a second transformation of my science identity.

The making of the altruistic scientist

In their study, Carlone and Johnson (2007: 1,188) quote an observation from Brickhouse (2001): 'Identity accounts for "individual agency as well as societal structures that constrain individual possibilities"'. I looked up the word 'agency' in a sociological context (remember I am a scientist) and the definition is 'the capacity of individuals to act independently and to make their own free choices' (Vermeesch and Crabbé, 2015: 1). Carlone and Johnson (2007: 1,210) go on to say that the stories of the women 'indicate that there is room for individual agency and cultural production at the university level'. The impact of individual agency, this ability to act independently, resonates strongly with me regarding the next stage of my journey of identity. Why? For many of the women in Carlone and Johnson's study, the experience of disruption did not 'derail' them from a career in science. My career was disrupted but I too stayed; I persisted for reasons I have articulated above.

The reasons for my staying, however, colluded to facilitate the further transformation of my science identity. Carlone and Johnson (2007: 1,199) call it the altruistic science identity – one that results from engaging in 'successful cultural productions', that is, a redefinition of whose recognition matters and for some what it means to be a woman of colour in science. The women in this group linked their pursuit of scientific competence to selfless goals and ambitions, 'using science in direct service of humanity' and wanting to 'give back to others' (1,199). Unlike those who identified with the research scientist, this group of women focused less on science for the sake of science and aligned themselves with altruism. This facilitated their persistence in science as it did not hinge on recognition by established meaningful scientific others, as it had for the research group. The sources of recognition were their communities and people of colour. Looking back, I realize that, at the beginning of my career as an academic scientist, part of my science identity did include an element of altruism. I too wanted to give back to my community, specifically to impact on the lives of upcoming Black men and women scientists. Wanting to give back to my community was a logical outcome of my upbringing and past experiences, influenced as they are by my race and gender. However, my altruism extended no further than thinking that just being present as a Black woman scientist was enough. The change resulting from the disruption of my science identity essentially altered my way of thinking.

Towards the end of the period of disrupted science identity, I took part in a study on women academics in which I articulated my frustrations. The interviewer, who is now a work colleague and friend, suggested I join my university's mentoring scheme as a mentee. Mentoring is often critiqued as premised on a deficit model – i.e. that people of colour lack the skills and confidence to succeed – rather than acknowledge institutionalized racism as the primary cause of racial disparities (Gabriel, 2016). Furthermore, it is used as a 'single target' approach (Armstrong and Jovanovic, 2015: 145) to address the under-representation of Black women in STEM. But such an approach fails to recognize the synergy between being Black and being a woman within the context of STEM in higher education (ibid.: 146). I accepted the opportunity to be mentored, fully aware that my disrupted science identity had nothing to do with any professional inadequacy and everything to do with an institutional structure that was impeding my progress because of my race and my gender.

My experience as a mentee afforded me new clarity. This clarity stemmed from realizing that my mentor's academic progress to professor was not via the route taken by many STEM academics – undergraduate degree to PhD to post-doctoral to lecturer – and that I had been blinded by a belief that there was only one way to progress, namely by adapting to the norms of the science environment, and that the recognition from important others was crucial to my self-recognition. Being mentored resulted in my redefining who I am as a Black woman scientist. Disrupted scientist has become altruistic scientist. I am now a scientist who gives back by focusing on my students' academic ambitions rather than my own. A scientist who will question and challenge decisions that do not benefit my students. A scientist who gives back by mentoring women scientists, Black and White, using my experience to aid in their progress. My students and my female peers are to me now meaningful others, to whom I turned for recognition and support. Transformed from disrupted to altruist, my fear, disillusionment, dented self-esteem and lack of direction dissipated and I found my voice as a Black woman scientist. Settles and colleagues (2007) found that women scientists who perceived that they had a voice had greater job satisfaction, and that their voice buffered a negative workplace climate. I believe that finding my voice has done even more than that: it has contributed to my recent successes.

Conclusion

My narrative clearly shows that my science identity is not fixed but dynamic. From research scientist to disrupted, and from disrupted to altruistic scientist, my identity change is a result of the interplay of my race and gender with the science environment. This fact acknowledged by Carlone and Johnson (2007) compelled me to reflect deeply on my science identity today. I recognize now that the altruist, although dominant, does not fully encompass my current science identity. I again see 'science as an exciting way of knowing' (Carlone and Johnson, 2007) and I have the recognition of established others, even though I do not actively seek it.

Thus, the research scientist has clearly returned and is now part of my science identity. I have a hybrid identity – an altruistic/research scientist born out of an experience that could have made me walk away from a discipline I love. Whether such a hybrid can exist within Carlone and Johnson's science identity model (2007) is unclear. They do acknowledge that some of the women in their study were able to 'work themselves into new trajectories', but offer no further analysis of these changes. However, the dynamism of the science identity means that it is highly improbable that my current science identity will remain fixed, since gender and race will continue to impact upon my experience in the science environment. I will, like the women in Carlone and Johnson's study (2007: 1,208), have to fight for my identity, 'performing, developing and achieving (it) again and again in different contexts and across time'.

On an intellectual level, the model that Carlone and Johnson (2007) developed has facilitated the articulation of my journey as a scientist in the context of my gender and race. On an emotional level, I believe that this articulation binds me to all the Black women scientists, past and present, who are fighting for recognition and are redefining their science identities within an environment and culture that presents itself as objective and as a meritocracy when it is in fact neither. It is clear that the science identity journey I have reflected upon is the result of this one single reality: I am, because of my gender and race, the living antithesis of the current 'embodiment of science' (Hirshfield and Joseph, 2012: 213) and 'the cultural stereotype of the scientist' (Settles *et al.*, 2007: 271).

This single reality is the reason why Black women are under-represented in science as researchers and academics, and I am not even talking about our presence, or lack of it, in positions of leadership (CaSE, 2014: 43; ECU, 2015: 278; Hill *et al.*, 2010: 68; Singh and Kwhali, 2015). The literature talks of subtle racism and the institutionalized, unconscious nature of racism coming into play when Black women scientists bid for recognition (Carlone and Johnson, 2007; Ramohai, 2014). The manifestations of this perpetual, subtle racism are pernicious: they deny Black women scientists their right to equality of opportunity, despite the clear benefits of inclusion and diversity (Fine and Handelsman, 2010; Universities UK, n.d.). Persistence born of my love of science was, ultimately, my weapon against the disruptive and destructive nature of this subtle racism, as my narrative illustrates, and I have no doubt that this love and persistence will be at the heart of my continued fight for my science identity.

References

Armstrong, M.A. and Jovanovic, J. (2015) 'Starting at the crossroads: Intersectional approaches to institutionally supporting underrepresented minority women STEM faculty'. *Journal of Women and Minorities in Science and Engineering*, 21 (2), 141–57.

Bhopal, K. (2016) 'Will the Race Equality Charter make the UK academy more diverse?'. *Times Higher Education*, 4 February. Online. www.timeshighereducation.com/blog/will-race-equality-charter-make-uk-academy-more-diverse (accessed 8 March 2017).

Brickhouse, N.W. (2001) 'Embodying science: A feminist perspective on learning'. *Journal of Research in Science Teaching*, 38 (3), 282–95.

Carlone, H.B. and Johnson, A. (2007) 'Understanding the science experiences of successful women of color: Science identity as an analytic lens'. *Journal of Research in Science Teaching*, 44 (8), 1187–218.

CaSE (Campaign for Science and Engineering) (2014) *Improving Diversity in STEM: A report by the Campaign for Science and Engineering (CaSE)*. London: CaSE. Online. http://sciencecampaign.org.uk/CaSEDiversityinSTEMreport2014.pdf (accessed 29 May 2015).

ECU (Equality Challenge Unit) (2015) *Equality in Higher Education: Statistical Report 2015 – Part 1: Staff*. London: Equality Challenge Unit. Online. www.ecu.ac.uk/wp-content/uploads/2015/11/Equality-in-HE-statistical-report-2015-part-1-staff.pdf (accessed 21 March 2016).

Else, H. (2014) 'BME scholars in science'. *Times Higher Education*, 17 April. Online. www.timeshighereducation.com/news/bme-scholars-in-science/2012740.article (accessed 8 March 2017).

— (2015) 'Academics from BME backgrounds squeezed out at the top'. *Times Higher Education*, 25 June. Online. www.timeshighereducation.com/academics-from-bme-backgrounds-squeezed-out-at-the-top (accessed 8 March 2017).

Fine, E. and Handelsman, J. (2010) *Benefits and Challenges of Diversity in Academic Settings*. 2nd ed. Madison: University of Wisconsin. Online. https://wiseli.engr.wisc.edu/docs/Benefits_Challenges.pdf (accessed 19 December 2016).

Gabriel, D. (2016) 'Will lack of career progression drive black female academics overseas?'. *Black British Academics*, 18 November. Online. http://blackbritishacademics.co.uk/2016/11/18/will-lack-of-career-progression-drive-black-female-academics-overseas (accessed 8 March 2017).

Grove, J. (2013) 'White academics "more likely to land professorships"'. *Times Higher Education*, 29 January. Online. www.timeshighereducation.com/news/white-academics-more-likely-to-land-professorships/2001154.article (accessed 8 March 2017).

— (2015) 'Black and ethnic minorities still have mountains to climb in higher education'. *Times Higher Education*, 5 November. Online. www.timeshighereducation.com/features/black-and-ethnic-minorities-still-have-mountains-to-climb-in-higher-education (accessed 8 March 2017).

— (2016) 'Universities confront "horrifying" figures on BME promotion'. *Times Higher Education*, 25 January. Online. www.timeshighereducation.com/news/universities-confront-horrifying-figures-bme-promotion (accessed 8 March 2017).

Hill, C., Corbett, C. and St. Rose, A. (2010) *Why So Few? Women in science, technology, engineering, and mathematics*. Washington, DC: American Association of University Women.

Hiraldo, P. (2010) 'The role of critical race theory in higher education'. *Vermont Connection*, 31, 53–9.

Hirshfield, L.E. and Joseph, T.D. (2012) '"We need a woman, we need a black woman": Gender, race, and identity taxation in the academy'. *Gender and Education*, 24 (2), 213–27.

Hunt, S. (2016) 'Racism in universities: "There is a sense your face doesn't fit"'. *The Guardian*, 4 February. Online. www.theguardian.com/higher-education-network/2016/feb/04/racism-in-universities-there-is-a-sense-your-face-doesnt-fit (accessed 8 March 2017).

Jones, C. (2006) 'Falling between the cracks: What diversity means for black women in higher education'. *Policy Futures in Education*, 4 (2), 145–59.

Lewis, B.F. (2006) *Content, Context, Currency, Critique and Conduct: A transformative prescription for African science education*. San Francisco: American Educational Research Association.

Malcom, S.M., Hall, P.Q. and Brown, J.W. (1976) *The Double Bind: The price of being a minority woman in science* (AAAS Report No. 76-R-3). Washington, DC: American Association for the Advancement of Science.

Mirza, H.S. (2006) 'Transcendence over diversity: Black women in the academy'. *Policy Futures in Education*, 4 (2), 101–13.

Morgan, W. (2016) 'Why is my professor still not black?'. *Times Higher Education*, 14 March. Online. www.timeshighereducation.com/blog/why-my-professor-still-not-black (accessed 8 March 2017).

Odoaje, F. (2014) 'Nigeria: Igbo's Ada as a tool for women empowerment'. *Folakemi*, 17 November. Online. https://folakemiodoaje.com/2014/11/17/igbos-ada (accessed 8 March 2017).

Parsons, E.R.C. and Mutegi, J.W. (2007) *Race Matters: Implications for science education*. New Orleans: National Association for Research in Science Teaching.

Ramohai, J. (2014) '"Marginalised access" in South African higher education: Black women academics speak!'. *Mediterranean Journal of Social Sciences*, 5 (20), 2976–85.

Reisz, M. (2015) 'Call to tackle lack of BME scholars in senior roles'. *Times Higher Education*, 18 June. Online. www.timeshighereducation.com/call-to-tackle-lack-of-bme-scholars-in-senior-roles (accessed 8 March 2017).

Rollock, N. (2016) 'How much does your university do for racial equality?'. *The Guardian*, 19 January. Online. www.theguardian.com/higher-education-network/2016/jan/19/how-much-does-your-university-do-for-racial-equality (accessed 8 March 2017).

Rousseau, D.M. (1988) 'The construction of climate in organizational research'. *International Review of Industrial and Organizational Psychology*, 3, 139–58.

Russell, M.L. and Atwater, M.M. (2005) 'Traveling the road to success: A discourse on persistence throughout the science pipeline with African American students at a predominantly white institution'. *Journal of Research in Science Teaching*, 42 (6), 691–715.

Seibert, S.E., Silver, S.R. and Randolph, W.A. (2004) 'Taking empowerment to the next level: A multiple-level model of empowerment, performance, and satisfaction'. *Academy of Management Journal*, 47 (3), 332–49.

Settles, I.H., Cortina, L.M., Stewart, A.J. and Malley, J. (2007) 'Voice matters: Buffering the impact of a negative climate for women in science'. *Psychology of Women Quarterly*, 31 (3), 270–81.

Singh, G. and Kwhali, J. (2015) *How Can We Make Not Break Black and Minority Ethnic Leaders in Higher Education?* (Stimulus Paper). London: Leadership Foundation for Higher Education.

Universities UK (n.d.) 'Inclusion, equality and diversity'. Online. www.universitiesuk.ac.uk/policy-and-analysis/Pages/inclusion-equality-diversity.aspx (accessed 19 December 2016).

Vermeesch, I. and Crabbé, A. (2015) 'Reflecting on structure and agency in deliberative governance approaches of transitions'. Panel session at the 10th International Conference in Interpretive Policy Analysis, Lille, France, 8–10 July 2015. Online. https://ipa2015.sciencesconf.org/conference/ipa2015/pages/Reflecting_on_structure_and_agency.pdf (accessed 20 December 2016).

Williams, R. (2013) 'The university professor is always White'. *The Guardian*, 28 January. Online. www.theguardian.com/education/2013/jan/28/women-bme-professors-academia (accessed 19 February 2016).

Wright, C., Thompson, S. and Channer, Y. (2007) 'Out of place: Black women academics in British universities'. *Women's History Review*, 16 (2), 145–62.

Chapter 10

Reclaiming freedom beyond the glass ceiling to transform institutional cultures

Aisha Richards

> *The importance of Black-led movements, which date back to the development of Black Consciousness during anti-colonialist struggles, should be respected.*
>
> (Bouattia, 2015: 25)

Introduction

In this chapter, I offer an autoethnographical narrative to articulate the ways in which I navigate academia through the prevalence of Whiteness (Fishkin, 1995), institutionally racist infrastructures (Lea, 2000) and individual practices that aimed to 'put me in my place' (Bagilhole, 2009; Bhopal and Jackson, 2013; Davies, 2011). I aim to highlight how the practice of Black feminism can be used for critical analysis while also shifting power away from the dominance of contemporary women's liberation struggle (Tree, 2010) to marginalized women. I present scenarios of how I have utilized the constructs of 'family' to circumvent and move beyond the hierarchical, gendered, racial and political structures coming from my community that view women as 'strategists and resilient social actors' (Rosaldo and Lamphere, 1974: 10). I also explore how, through the contributions of Black women extending beyond our immediate families, we practise 'mutual aid', which offers emotional support, economic supplements and most importantly protects our family's integrity from assault by external forces (McAdoo, 1980; Gregory, 1999). I have cultivated family networks to feed my need for supportive environments within the academic setting, which give me support and strength and help me to navigate through the learning of others in an often stressful and competitive academic environment (Gregory, 1999).

Teaching practice as a catalyst for empowerment

I don't generally call myself an academic; rather a teacher and creative practitioner who has practised pedagogies of social justice at my institution for more than 15 years. Social justice pedagogy is a framework that challenges the status quo (Nagda *et al.*, 2003) and has direct affiliations to inclusive learning and teaching. It refers to the ways in which pedagogy, curricula and assessment are designed and delivered to engage students in learning that is meaningful, relevant and accessible to all (Hockings, 2010) while also being steeped in the Freirean theories and practices of liberation through education. The word 'academic' is coded to me in many ways, as the surprise on people's faces when I state that I am one suggests I do not meet their expectations. This could be due to the historical and social constructs that mean that the Black British female academic has low cultural and academic value within the sector (ECU, 2009).

The under-representation of Black and minority ethnic staff is prevalent (Beattie *et al.*, 2013) and I work within the art, design and communication fields that are starkly White. This is evidenced through creative arts and design subjects having the second-largest discrepancy between White academics and those of colour, with a mere 3.6 per cent representation (ECU, 2009). Additionally, art and design has the second-largest attainment gap across the higher education sector: 31 per cent of Black British Caribbean and Black British African students gain a good degree (first or upper second) compared with 64 per cent of White students (Woodfield, 2014; Finnigan and Richards, 2016). Consequently, as a teacher I am acutely aware that the historical constructs and structures of oppression and marginalization sit both inside and outside my institution and affect both staff and students. Black feminists conceptualize education as the practice of freedom (hooks, 1994) for marginalized communities, which then produces a safe space for all students to grow. My work is influenced by Freire (2000), so aims to help students to develop consciousness of freedom, recognize authoritarian tendencies, and connect knowledge to power and the ability to take constructive action (Giroux, 2010). This creates an interconnectivity between history and the present day, inspires changemakers and promotes a consciousness of the constructs that oppress particular groups in many different ways.

In my 15 years of teaching on a master's course, my students have produced a full spectrum of outcomes, from a travel book on the 'real' London, which documents the voices of a variety of Londoners for the Korean market (and continues to be a best-seller in South Korea), to tools for developing countries to teach science, technology, engineering, arts and maths (currently several non-governmental organizations are implementing this product), and everything in between. I feel empowered by my diverse student population and gain a great deal of learning from their narratives and how these inform and connect meaningfully with their research areas. Through the inspiration of my students, I have developed a number of strategies to support the embedding of pedagogies of social justice into teaching practice. One of these is the co-creation and joint management of the Postgraduate Certificate in Education unit called Inclusive Practice in Higher Education. What is born out of pedagogies of social justice is a form of 'co-intentionality' – that is, mutual intentions – which makes the study collectively owned (Shor, 1993: 26). This practice values my Black female perspective and my experience of counter-storytelling to share and grow. Although my experience is classed as an outsider perspective that counters the normalized experiences of women, it allows a way of destroying dominant group perspectives that legitimize social exclusion (Ladson-Billings, 1996), using narratives that are steeped in critical race feminism theories (Tree, 2010) to explore issues of dominance in educational settings.

Although I have been an associate lecturer since 2002, my key milestones came between 2008 and 2010, when my experiences at work were challenging, to say the least. But these were also the most profoundly important years of my academic career. Research suggests that academic staff of colour who are as qualified as their White counterparts are often overlooked for promotion and are not encouraged to apply for senior positions (ECU, 2009; Bhopal and Jackson, 2013). Within higher education, 45 per cent of academics in the UK are women (Black and Islam, 2014), but 89 per cent of these women are White. Black women account for just 2.2 per cent of all staff within higher education (ECU, 2013) and only 30 of the 110 Black professors in 2013/14 were women (Black British Academics, 2016). The data and discussions around women in academia do not begin to address the presence or lack of Black British women academics, or the complex impact of this disparity. However, through our narratives within this book, we may begin to shed further light.

In 2008, I applied for research funding to explore the experiences and career trajectories of students of colour. My course leader refused to sign the funding application, sending a lengthy email stating that I was 'too inexperienced to deliver the research on my own'. However, I realized that, as an associate lecturer, I did not need their agreement as I could deliver this investigation outside my teaching hours. Accordingly, I applied and was awarded a grant. I completed the research in 2009 and the outcomes were like a magnifying glass showing up the relationship with students of colour and arts sectors through testimony. Storytelling is not merely for entertainment; it is also an educational tool, and for many, it is a way of life. For some, it is the only way to comprehend, analyse and deal with life

(Amoah, 1997). The stories of these participants were extremely powerful, both for me as the researcher and – I believe – for the sector, even if it was not ready to listen. In my mind, I was moving from silence into speech, and moving beyond the colonized and the exploited (hooks, 1981; Griffin, 2012) into a space of liberation for marginalized students and a Black female academic within this environment.

This freedom inspired me to suggest to senior management that we take action before the information found its way to the press. My suggestion was met with hostility and fear. 'Are you planning on going to the press, Aisha? You know if you do you will never work in education or the creative sector again,' one senior manager warned me after a meeting about my research findings. This came as a real shock, since it was said by a self-declared feminist involved in widening participation research. While (White) feminists claim to expose gendered discrimination (Pollock, 2003), this framework often excludes the experiences, stories of oppression and struggles of Black women (Carby, 1997; hooks, 1994). Black feminism aims to address this disparity, while capturing intersectional experiences (Crenshaw, 1991) that focus on the specific context of the experiences (Carby, 1997; Young, 2000). Thus, I share my experiences as a Black British female academic – from a position explained through Black feminist theory about the reality of being one of the most economically, socially and politically disadvantaged groups nationally and globally (Mohanty, 2003; Nandi and Platt, 2010; Mirza, 2015).

Many of the subtle threats to me from White women have only come to light in recent years. Rather than understanding that what I was suggesting was for the benefit of the students, alumni and our institution, this was instead perceived as a threat, and I was told I was naïve. Power was at play.

My colleagues mistrusted me and questioned my credibility when I applied for further research funding, and this continues to the present day. The same course leader who had tried to obstruct my first research application was again involved and my Dean refused to sign my new application. The title of this study was 'Black Alchemy: To what extent do personal and professional development components within the creative curriculum affect the achievement and progression of Black students into successful creative careers?' The title was deemed controversial 'for all sorts of reasons', including, as highlighted in my feedback, using the word 'Black'. Even the mentorship of a notable academic within my institution and their support for my application was not enough to gain me teaching and professional fellowship funding. The administrator of the fund noted the line manager's obstructive behaviour but submitted my application anyway, with a note stating that I 'did not have my line manager's support'. The administrator told me that in the years of managing funding schemes within the institution, a line manager failing to support their team member was unheard of.

Reflecting on this dark time still makes me angry. But I hold my head high. I believe that I am worth standing up for in a world that crudely tells me otherwise (Griffin, 2012)! While applying for funding, I had started developing a business plan for a race equality programme called Shades of Noir (SoN). As you can imagine, my relationship with my course director deteriorated during this time and since. They undermined me with my peers and students, and even tried to instigate a disciplinary case against me. My line manager's behaviour appears characteristic of what distributed leadership theory (Lumby, 2013) calls the invisibility of discriminatory practices. My line manager's line manager was no help either. Just as a child shuts her eyes to remove a threat by making it invisible, so distributed leadership removes inequality 'ontologically' (ibid.: 24). It was as though my line managers were doing everything possible to silence me and the voices of the marginalized that I sought to capture through the research.

I drew strength and advice from my family and I started building my 'professional family' of staff members across my institution. I later brought a senior manager to my disciplinary meeting (which I had previously been unaware was my right). The surprise on the faces of the course leader and senior lecturer conducting the disciplinary meeting when we walked into the meeting was priceless. I witnessed in that moment a shift in power that gave me the strength to challenge the grounds of the disciplinary, which was successfully overturned. At that moment I understood what Paulo Freire (2000) meant when he spoke of the oppressed being the motivating force for liberating action.

The development of mutual aid to support academic activism

Although I was denied the second funding award, I was still working actively on the development of SoN. During this time, I sought advice from elders within our staff community group. This group, GEMS (Group for the Equality of Minority Staff), became a crucial source of support and political empowerment. With more than 100 members, including over one-third of the staff of colour, it is the largest and longest-standing staff network in our institution, established more than 20 years ago. GEMS is an autonomous network, providing a safe space for staff of colour to share experiences and develop action plans, and it has a history of Black female leadership. I have relied on GEMS for support and collaboration. Cultural safety and the creation of safe spaces include those actions and environments that recognize and respect the cultural identity of others and take account of their needs and rights (Hill, 1991; Anderson *et al.*, 2003). I learnt from the elders that my experience of obstructions to my progression was not unique and that White women, especially those in middle management, would smile warmly while perpetrating a multitude of micro-aggressions, including appropriating the work of people of colour.

I also learnt that the institution did not value our contribution, or recognize the prejudicial practices it deploys, and that this had a devastating impact on staff of colour. 'Don't trust the institution but we are here to support you' was GEM's message. I did not take the message lightly – my mantra has always been that the lessons of the past should lay the foundations for future resistance (Amoah, 1997). Importantly, as individuals within our staff community, GEMS members don't always agree – we learn from each other and benefit from different perspectives. However, we do share common experiences and there is solidarity and sisterhood, which has created a unified political voice that contributes powerfully to addressing prejudicial practices by challenging the institutional culture.

With the support of GEMS, and my experience as a teacher and a graduate of the institution, I completed my SoN proposal and presented it to the diversity team and key heads of department. The proposal made it clear that I owned the concept, that it was an external proposal and was designed primarily to support creative academia in the delivery of pedagogies of social justice. Remarkably, the university's diversity team and heads of department were utterly dismissive, although I was aware that some limited examples of Black-led programmes existed within the institution or across the sector. However, I continued to be explicit both in the documentation and my articulation of the importance of Black-led movements, dating back to the Black consciousness movement during anti-colonialist struggles (Bouattia, 2015). It was crucial to highlight that students of colour are less likely than Whites to find role models among faculty staff and how this may contribute to the likelihood of finding diversity included as part of their intellectual experience of university (Bhagat and O'Neill, 2011), and how this links to the retention, attainment and experience of these students.

I was told that I was being called an activist within the institution. On reflection, maybe I could have articulated the information in a different way, to reduce the close personal involvement I have with the data and the impact on mind, body and soul of the staff and students who look like me;

but I was angry. I was disappointed and I wanted everyone to know a truth. These statistics are steeped in history and affect people's lives, their futures. I really began to understand what Black feminism is and how it can provide the understanding and strength needed to make decisions rooted in social justice. Thus, I not only stand by my decision to develop SoN, I stand too with Rachel Alicia Griffin:

> For those who are angry right alongside me, I welcome your presence and can only hope that this article helps strengthen your determined embrace of autoethnographic writing as a means of resistance. This work is dedicated to every woman of color who has had to bite her tongue so hard that it bleeds to protect her body, mind, soul, loved ones, livelihood, or even her life.
>
> (Griffiin, 2012: 139)

Maybe it is this anger that caused me to seek 'mutual aid' (McAdoo, 1980; Gregory, 1999) from family structures, as I did. I believe it was my anger that motivated me to persevere with parties within my institution, which ultimately led to a meeting with the Dean of Students, with whom I could talk through the rejection of my funding application. During this constructive discussion, I asserted that SoN was the only way I knew to begin the necessary progression towards institutional change in creative arts education and industry.

Driving institutional change through collective action

Shades of Noir is now eight years old (in 2017) and funded mainly by University of the Arts London. However, it continues to be owned by me, is separated from my contracted teaching hours and provides a valuable service to higher education institutions. It is currently in its fourth phase, each one having had a different team of academics, recent graduates and students. Crucially, they support the next steps, deliverables and media for implementation through critical reflection that moves beyond the additive approach to pedagogy. SoN avoids an additive approach where tokenistic additions are made to the curriculum that fail to help students view society from diverse cultural and ethnic perspectives and to understand the ways in which the histories and cultures of the nation's diverse ethnic, racial, cultural and religious groups are inextricably bound (Banks, 1989). Through the formation of SoN, I have created an additional family-type structure, which generates space for mutual aid and responds directly to student demands to liberate the curriculum (Ali *et al.*, 2011).

Changing its personnel every 18 months has been an important strategy, helping to protect the physical and emotional well-being of SoN team members. My first team experienced discrimination, both raced and gendered, micro-aggressions and direct abuse, creating a weighty burden of responsibility for me. However, the team's loyalty to supporting social justice pedagogy and institutional change meant that they were willing to keep pushing even though it was painful. While working on her PhD thesis, one member of phase one put her public relations and journalistic expertise to use when the university communications team tried to gain media control of the first all-Black alumni exhibition within the institution – and failed. I am forever indebted to her and all of the past SoN contributors. Many have gone on to do amazing things.

Managing and leading the SoN programme has not been easy, and I still tread carefully through Whiteness within institutions, especially when there is talk of diversity and equality. I have experienced challenge after challenge and continue to be tested. But I try to reclaim my power and retain my sanity by calling out oppressive practices. For example, I sent an email to a senior staff member with only two years' service in my institution:

> As you are leaving I will not be presenting a formal complaint
> of racism through consistent micro-aggressions. However, at this
> stage I think you should know that I find your repeated actions
> that seem to only target 'me' as the only Black person in the team,
> highly disgraceful.

As a methodology, autoethnography aims to embrace subjectivity, engage critical self-reflexivity, speak rather than be spoken for, interrogate power and resist oppression (Griffin, 2012). It is this that allows me to argue that senior management new to my institution fail to understand the history, journey and position that I and the SoN team have earned based on its continued quality and innovative approaches to education and social justice. We struggle to evolve our learnt practices of oppression, and this is highly stressful.

Black feminism brings home the reality of Blackness (Fanon, 1986) and its endeavour to reveal the ways in which 'race' – inextricably linked with gender, class and sexuality – still matters in our organizational structures, both symbolically and as part of our political story (Mirza, 2015). This is the reality of my experience, of being continually tested and challenged by fairly new appointees to senior posts. Race and gender are largely ignored in literature on educational leadership, and distributed leadership is no exception (Lumby, 2013). Therefore, raced and gendered discrimination that manifests in subtle day-to-day practices is largely invisible and goes unnoticed, except to those of us who experience it. This compounds our sense of being undervalued as women of colour. Black feminism not only challenges race, gender and class oppression but empowers us as women of colour (Amoah, 1997), and as Black British female academics. Black women are key figures in developing survival strategies, from past periods of slavery and colonialism to present-day resistance of racism within our institutions by creating spaces for us to speak (Carby, 1997; Young, 2000). The challenges I encountered, in trying to gain funding for research to examine the experience of students of colour so we can develop pedagogical solutions, are not unique. Overall, Black and minority ethnic staff have fewer opportunities to develop research (ECU, 2009; Jones, 2006; Wright *et al.*, 2007).

This realization motivated me to stand for election and serve as co-chair of GEMS for two terms over a four-year period. I have worked tirelessly to grow our membership by 100 per cent, and to ensure that staff of colour have a powerful, collective voice and representation in spaces where we are usually excluded. I was elected as a member of the Academic Board and have served on numerous committees. Through 'having a seat at the table' I have lobbied on behalf of staff of colour for changes to policy and practice.

Conclusion

In this chapter, I have reflected on some of my experiences as a Black British female academic so as to highlight the invisibility of raced and gendered discriminatory practices. I hope my contribution helps to stir people into action. Given the dominance of Whiteness in positions of power and its record on raced and gendered discrimination, I hope that those in positions of power within and beyond my institution pay attention. The action I am advocating is multi-faceted, entailing:

- actively listening to marginalized voices, followed by ongoing consultation on current practices and proposed changes;
- maintaining safe spaces for staff and students of colour to foster self-care and mental well-being;
- promoting leadership among the marginalized that enables participation in decision-making processes – which may mean stepping aside from positions of power and privilege; and
- accepting that, as Black women academics, we own our narratives and have expertise through our lived experience and therefore that

writing about us or our work without our collaboration, consent or recognition is a form of appropriation.

The type of actions I describe characterize the role of allies, and over the years I have developed important relationships with allies at various levels in my institution. With mutual respect and trust, these allies have taken the actions described, and continue to challenge themselves and remain reflective. They have become part of my 'professional family'. We don't always agree, but they do have my back while understanding that the cause is bigger than we are, or than our institution.

References

Ali, U., Baars, V., Bailey, A., Hart, E., Kaur, R. and Sesay, K. (2011) *Liberation, Equality, and Diversity in the Curriculum*. London: NUS. Online. www.staffs.ac.uk/assets/NUS%20Liberation%20Equality%20and%20Diversity%20in%20the%20Curriculum%202011_tcm44-65179.pdf (accessed 10 December 2016).

Amoah, J. (1997) 'Narrative: The road to black feminist theory'. *Berkeley Women's Law Journal*, 12 (1), 84–102.

Anderson, J., Perry, J., Blue, C., Browne, A., Henderson, A., Khan, K.B., Kirkham, S.R., Lynam, J., Semeniuk, P. and Smye, V. (2003) '"Rewriting" cultural safety within the postcolonial and postnational feminist project: Toward new epistemologies of healing'. *Advances in Nursing Science*, 26 (3), 196–214.

Bagilhole, B. (2009) *Understanding Equal Opportunities and Diversity: The social differentiations and intersections of inequality*. Bristol: Policy Press.

Banks, J.A. (1989) 'Approaches to multicultural curriculum reform'. *Trotter Review*, 3 (3), 17–19.

Beattie, G., Cohen, D. and McGuire, L. (2013) 'An exploration of possible unconscious ethnic biases in higher education: The role of implicit attitudes on selection for university posts'. *Semiotica*, 197, 171–201.

Bhagat, D. and O'Neill, P. (eds) (2011) *Inclusive Practices, Inclusive Pedagogies: Learning from widening participation research in art and design higher education*. London: Council for Higher Education in Art and Design. Online. http://guildhe.ac.uk/ukadia/wp-content/uploads/sites/3/2013/11/Inclusive_Practices_Inclusive_Pedagogies.pdf (accessed 29 July 2017).

Bhopal, K. and Jackson, J. (2013) *The Experiences of Black and Minority Ethnic Academics: Multiple identities and career progression*. Southampton: University of Southampton.

Black British Academics (2016) 'HESA statistics professors by race and gender'. Online. http://blackbritishacademics.co.uk/focus/hesa-statistics-professors-by-race-and-gender (accessed 29 July 2017).

Black, C. and Islam, A. (2014) 'Women in academia: What does it take to reach the top?'. *The Guardian*, 24 February. Online. www.theguardian.com/higher-education-network/blog/2014/feb/24/women-academia-promotion-cambridge (accessed 18 March 2017).

Bouattia, M. (2015) 'Beyond the gap: Dismantling institutional racism, decolonising education'. In Alexander, C. and Arday, J. (eds) *Aiming Higher: Race, inequality and diversity in the academy*. London: Runnymede Trust, 24–6.

Carby, H.V. (1997) 'White woman listen! Black feminism and the boundaries of sisterhood'. In Mirza, H.S. (ed.) *Black British Feminism: A reader*. London: Routledge, 45–53.

Crenshaw, K. (1991) 'Mapping the margins: Intersectionality, identity politics, and violence against women of color'. *Stanford Law Review*, 43, 1241–99.

Davies, E.M. (2011) *Women on Boards: An independent review into women on boards*. London: Department for Business, Innovation and Skills.

ECU (Equality Challenge Unit) (2009) *The Experience of Black and Minority Ethnic Staff Working in Higher Education*. London: Equality Challenge Unit.

— (2013) *Equality in Higher Education: Statistical report 2013*. London: Equality Challenge Unit.

Fanon, F. (1986) *Black Skin, White Masks*. London: Pluto Press.

Finnigan, T. and Richards, A. (2016) 'Retention and attainment in the disciplines: Art and design'. York: Higher Education Academy. Online. www.heacademy. ac.uk/sites/default/files/ug_retention_and_attainment_in_art_and_design2.pdf (accessed 10 December 2016).

Fishkin, S.F. (1995) 'Interrogating "whiteness", complicating "blackness": Remapping American culture'. *American Quarterly*, 47 (3), 428–66.

Freire, P. (2000) *Pedagogy of the Oppressed*. Trans. Ramos, M.B. New York: Continuum.

Giroux, H.A. (2010) 'Lessons from Paulo Freire'. *Chronicle of Higher Education*, 17 October. Online. www.chronicle.com/article/Lessons-From-Paulo-Freire/124910 (accessed 29 July 2017).

Gregory, S.T. (1999) *Black Women in the Academy: The secrets to success and achievement*. Rev. ed. Lanham, MD: University Press of America.

Griffin, R.A. (2012) 'I AM an angry Black woman: Black feminist autoethnography, voice, and resistance'. *Women's Studies in Communication*, 35 (2), 138–57.

Hill, P. (ed.) (1991) *Cultural Safety Hui of the Whanau Kawa Whakaruruhau, Apumoana Marae, Rotorua, June 30–July 4 1991*. Palmerston North: PSI Solutions.

Hockings, C. (2010) *Inclusive Learning and Teaching in Higher Education: A synthesis of research*. York: Higher Education Academy. Online. www. heacademy.ac.uk/sites/default/files/inclusive_teaching_and_learning_in_he_ synthesis_200410_0.pdf (accessed 12 December 2016).

hooks, b. (1981) *Ain't I a Woman: Black women and feminism*. Boston: South End Press.

— (1994) *Teaching to Transgress: Education as the practice of freedom*. New York: Routledge.

Jones, C. (2006) 'Falling between the cracks: What diversity means for black women in higher education'. *Policy Futures in Education*, 4 (2), 145–59.

Ladson-Billings, G.J. (1996) 'Lifting as we climb: The womanist tradition in multicultural education'. In Banks, J.E. (ed.) *Multicultural education, transformative knowledge and action*. New York: Teachers College Press, 179–200.

Lea, J. (2000) 'The Macpherson Report and the question of institutional racism'. *Howard Journal of Criminal Justice*, 39 (3), 219–33.

Lumby, J. (2013) 'Distributed leadership: The uses and abuses of power'. *Educational Management Administration and Leadership*, 41 (5), 581–97.

McAdoo, H.P. (1980) 'Black mothers and the extended family support network'. In Rodgers-Rose, L.F. (ed.) *The Black Woman*. Beverly Hills, CA: SAGE Publications, 125–44.

Mirza, H.S. (2015) '"Harvesting our collective intelligence": Black British feminism in post-race times'. *Women's Studies International Forum*, 51, 1–9.

Mohanty, C.T. (2003) *Feminism without Borders: Decolonizing theory, practicing solidarity*. Durham, NC: Duke University Press.

Nagda, B.R.A., Gurin, P. and Lopez, G.E. (2003) 'Transformative pedagogy for democracy and social justice'. *Race Ethnicity and Education*, 6 (2), 165–91.

Nandi, A. and Platt, L. (2010) *Ethnic Minority Women's Poverty and Economic Well Being*. London: Government Equalities Office.

Pollock, G. (2003) *Vision and Difference: Feminism, femininity and the histories of art*. London: Routledge.

Rosaldo, M.Z. and Lamphere, L. (eds) (1974) *Woman, Culture, and Society*. Stanford, CA: Stanford University Press.

Shor, I. (1993) 'Paulo Freire's critical pedagogy'. In McLaren, P. and Leonard, P. (eds) *Paulo Freire: A critical encounter*. London: Routledge, 25–35.

Tree, G.G. (2010) 'Critical race feminism as outsider method: Personal praxis as critical pedagogy'. In Hill, K., Horwood, K., Jones, S. and Koens, K. (eds) *Methodology: Innovative approaches to research*. Leeds: Leeds Metropolitan University, 11–13.

Woodfield, R. (2014) *Undergraduate Retention and Attainment across the Disciplines*. York: Higher Education Academy.

Wright, C., Thompson, S. and Channer, Y. (2007) 'Out of place: Black women academics in British universities'. *Women's History Review*, 16 (2), 145–62.

Young, L. (2000) 'What is black British feminism?'. *Women: A Cultural Review*, 11 (1–2), 45–60.

Conclusion

Deborah Gabriel

As ten women of colour in British academia, we bared our souls in service to Black feminism, fellow academics, women of colour in other areas of employment – and to our institutions. While reflectively analysing our raced and gendered experiences has been a cathartic process, it has also been painful to recollect and re-live what were, at the time, difficult episodes in our lives. However, these challenging reflections afforded us the opportunity to acknowledge how far we have come. The subtitle of this book – Narratives of women of colour surviving and thriving in British academia – points to a focus on 'survival' and success, in terms of 'thriving'. But while the experiences of marginalization, exclusion, racial and sexual abuse, unbelonging and denied opportunities are easy to identify, the successes may not be obvious to all our readers. As part of our 'self-valuation' and 'self-definition' (Collins, 1989) we do not allude to 'thriving' in terms of career progression – since collectively our goal is equality and social justice. We therefore speak of 'thriving' with regards to our emotional and spiritual growth and development, our endurance, determination and perseverance in our ambition to be agents of change in our various roles within and beyond our institutions. While we seek race and gender equality within academia, we pursue this goal not solely for improving our own experiences. Since raced and gendered ideologies, attitudes and behaviours are channelled through and within higher education – we hope that by tackling racial inequality in academia we also combat racial inequality in the wider society.

Collins (1990: 221) argues that 'new knowledge is important for social change', and that social transformation occurs when individuals develop the critical consciousness to change the nature of the relations that govern oppression and resistance. We hope that this book is read widely and at all levels, from students to vice chancellors and Board directors and everyone in between – as everyone has the power to make a contribution to wider change. Readership must be wider than those working in equality and diversity roles, who often bear sole responsibility within universities for promoting race and gender equality. It is everyone's responsibility to promote and deliver race and gender equality and stand up to all forms of discrimination. We believe our book belongs on desks everywhere and should be read and discussed openly in discussions that may sometimes cause discomfort, but these are the discussions that need to take place to share our knowledge in ways that promote the learning and growth that will achieve lasting institutional cultural change.

References

Collins, P.H. (1989) 'The social construction of black feminist thought'. *Signs: Journal of Women in Culture and Society*, 14 (4), 745–73.

— (1990) *Black Feminist Thought: Knowledge, consciousness, and the politics of empowerment.* London: Routledge.

Index

Index